IDONAPSHE
Let's Eat
TRADITIONAL ZUNI FOODS

ZUNI A:SHIWI PUBLISHING, LTD.

A:SHIWI A:WAN MUSEUM AND HERITAGE CENTER

THE UNIVERSITY OF NEW MEXICO PRESS, ALBUQUERQUE

IDONAPSHE
Let's Eat
TRADITIONAL ZUNI FOODS

Stories and recipes compiled by

Rita Edaakie, Tradition Bearer

A:shiwi A:wan Museum and Heritage Center

Library of Congress Cataloging-in-Publication Data

Edaakie, Rita.
Idonapshe / Let's eat: traditional Zuni foods:
stories and recipes / compiled by Rita Edaakie.
p.   cm.
Includes index.
ISBN 0-8263-2046-5 (paper)
1. Cookery, American—Southwestern style.
2. Indian cookery.
3. Cookery—New Mexico.
4. Zuni Indians—Social life and customs.
I. Title
TX715.2.S69E33   1999
641.59′2979—dc21   98-43574
                                                      CIP

CONTENTS

South side of Zuni Pueblo. Courtesy of the Smithsonian Institution.
Photo by Timothy H. O'Sullivan.

ACKNOWLEDGMENTS

This book would not have been possible without the help and support of many Zuni community members and others.

Thanks to Lolita Edaakie, Margaret Edaakie, Vera Laweka, Alice Natewa, Frances Wytsalucy, and other "elderlies" of the Zuni Senior Center for their wonderful stories and recipes. Thanks to Cindy Waseta, a summer JTPA (Job Training Partnership Act) intern and student at Zuni High School, Georgia Epaloose, and Marvella Epaloose for reading and correcting several drafts of the recipes and stories.

The Zuni language alphabet has only existed since the 1970's and the rules of grammar and spelling continue to be developed. Thanks to Edward Wemytewa of the Zuni Rainbow Project, Wilfred Eriacho Sr. of the Zuni Public School District Bilingual Program, Ben Kallestewa, and Paul Neha for correcting our translations of Zuni into English and making sure our Zuni was spelled correctly.

Thanks to Raelynn Cachini and Fernandez Amesoli, both Service Learning students from Twin Buttes High School, Clayton Edaakie, a Zuni High School student, and Edward Wemytewa for their wonderful artwork. Thanks to Gwyneria Isaac and Wendy Fontenelle for their help in researching the historic photographs and to Guy Prouty for the front cover photo. Thanks to the Smithsonian Institution for providing the Zuni community with copies of the photographs of Zuni housed at the Smithsonian.

Thanks to Louise Ingraham and the Zuni Diabetes Prevention Program for providing the dietary analysis of many of our recipes.

Rita Edaakie, Tradition Bearer
A:shiwi A:wan Museum and Heritage Center

Anne E. Beckett, Executive Director
Zuni A:shiwi Publishing

FOREWORD

Ever since our ancestors stopped gathering plants and began nurturing crops, the diet of Zunis has reflected the environment, hardships, and necessities required to survive in a high arid climate. As we learned to survive in what we call the Middle Place, our food also became a sacred element for offering gratitude and respect to our ancestors. In essence partaking of food is more than a matter of physical sustenance, it is also a personal ritual to honor the long history of our people, which is a story intimate and dense with meaning.

In the household setting, the preparation of food is a broad gender and intergenerational undertaking. Men and boys spend days in Zuni's backcountry cutting large supplies of firewood while mothers, sisters, and patriarchal aunts work for what seems to be endless hours preparing meals in large kitchens or stew houses as has been the tradition for centuries. Essentially, the art of food preparation is the women's crafting and it is in Zuni kitchens that food can actually take on the personality and reputation of the cook. In fact some say the spicier a dish is ... well, you'll just have to ask a Zuni what this says about a cook. The kitchen is also the traditional meeting place of Zuni women, where family news, community gossip, and drop-jaw teasing occurs without restraint!

The original crops grown at Zuni, ino:dena do:sho: demɬanahna:we, were more plentiful in past years and back then, were the only source of crops for many centuries. But due to influences such as the introduction of a cash economy, wars, changes in land tenure and so on, these ancient crops steadily became less abundant and less common in the Zuni daily diet. Eventually piki bread, blue marbles, and bean stew became only special occasion dishes. With the introduction of modern ingredients like mutton, wheat, sugar, lard, and coffee, the diet of Zunis changed dramatically. Our bodies, which had adapted to marathon work-days in the fields and the occasional hard times when crops were scarce, became susceptible to the new availability of sugars and fats and the diseases that accompany them.

Recognizing the essential goodness of our original crops and their present scarcity led to a recent resurgence of farming these old crops again. Today a small community seedbank stores and makes available old-style variety seeds for Zuni farmers, and a Zuni Organic Farmers Cooperative has an equipment rental program to allow limited-resource farmers a chance to break ground and cultivate old family fields again. As more of the original ingredients become available from farming, the closer we will be to our lands and the healthier we will be.

The recipes and anecdotes in this book come from the hearts and experiences of Zuni cooks. By publishing this book we have learned how the broad canvas of old and new cooking styles is an enlightening story of Zuni social and cultural adaptation. This book is also a response to the contemporary Zuni question, "how do you make … ?" The recipes in this book will no doubt be a practical resource for cooks, but if you read and imagine, you might hear grandma's shuffling feet on the wrinkled linoleum floor at daybreak, crackling fires in woodstoves, children's voices, and elders speaking archaic Zuni telling how it was and how it should be.

Jim Enote
Pueblo of Zuni

Jim Enote serves on the board of directors of the A:shiwi A:wan Museum and Heritage Center and Zuni A:shiwi Publishing and is the director of the Zuni Conservation Project.

Rita Edaakie (right) and her granddaughter, Breanna
Edaakie, baking bread. Dowa Yalanne (Corn Mountain) is
in the background. Photo courtesy of Guy Prouty.

An Introduction To The Zuni Language

The Zuni language has existed since the Zuni people emerged into the Fourth World. As far back as Zuni memory goes this has been the language of the Zuni people. Unlike most languages that belong to a family of languages, such as English belonging to the Germanic languages, Zuni is a language isolate. It is unrelated to any known language, including those spoken by its Rio Grande pueblo neighbors and the Hopi people.

Zuni is a living language and is spoken by Zuni people today. The amount of Zuni spoken and the overall quality of the language have been affected by the introduction of other languages, most notably Spanish and English. With the Spanish settlers came new foods such as chiles, peaches, cilantro, wheat, and domesticated sheep. The Zuni people either invented new words or incorporated the Spanish and English words into their vocabulary to be able to speak about these new things, and this practice continues today.

Religious efforts to strengthen the Zuni language take place in the kiva and through the fraternities. There are secular efforts within the community to revitalize the language: the Zuni Public School District's Bilingual Program provides instruction conducted in the Zuni language at all grade levels; *The Shiwi Messenger*, Zuni's community newspaper, regularly features articles written in Zuni, Idiwanan An Chawe, a Zuni language theater, writes and performs plays on stage and radio; and the A:shiwi A:wan Museum and Heritage Center creates Zuni language exhibits. Over time the community has audio-recorded many elderly Zuni people to establish a resource of old spoken Zuni.

Like all the indigenous languages of North America, Zuni only recently became a written language. Previously, all the Zuni stories, histories, and beliefs were passed down orally from one generation to another. The invention of an alphabet in the 1970's provided the necessary symbols for writing down the language. Written language creates another way to share knowledge and preserve the language, but it also forces a certain amount of standardization.

THE ZUNI ALPHABET:

The Zuni alphabet is a phonetic alphabet. Although the Zuni alphabet is adopted from the English, there are several characters not included: f, g, j, P, q, r, T, v, x, and z. Several different characters have been added as well: **ch'**, **'**, **:**, **k'**, **ł**, **Ts**, and **ts'**. Some of these sounds are difficult to pronounce by English speakers.

Two letters, p and t, can be found in the middle of a word but they can never initiate a word. A glottal stop (') coupled with a **ch**, **k**, and **ts** is sometimes referred to as "popped," as sound is forced by air built up at the back of the mouth. A glottal stop (') after a vowel shortens the duration of sound, and a colon (:) after a vowel doubles its sound in length. A colon (:) is only used after vowels, but a glottal stop (') after a consonant, usually at the end of a syllable, *abruptly stops the sound.*

The slash l (ł) sound is sometimes written in the form **lth**, but the sound is produced by saying the **l** and **th** simultaneously. The tongue is pressed against the soft palate and air is directed on either side of it.

EXAMPLES OF ZUNI PRONUNCIATION AND TRANSLATION:

Idonapshe
> **ee**-doe-knop-shay
> Let's eat!

Hebok'o:muwe
> hay-bow-kgoh-**moo**-way—the "bow" is pronounced like bow and arrow. (The **kg** sound is very quick and sharp.)
> Sourdough Bread—plural

Ts'upbachi
> **tsuep**-bah-chee—the t and the s are pronounced together quick and sharp, the p is very soft.
> Yucca Fruit Bananas

Ko'lehoł K'ola A:wakk'yana'dun'ona
>
> **ko**-lay-holth /**kgo**-la / ahhh-wok-kgya-nah-**dune**-own-nah
>
> How To Roast Green Chiles

Sumapbo:we
>
> **sue**-mop-boe-way—lengthen the "boe" sound.
>
> A liquid dish not necessarily the same as soup—plural

Woleyanne
>
> **woe**-lay-ahn-nay
>
> Stew—singular

K'ola K'yałk'osenne
>
> **kgo**-la / **kg-ahlth-co**-sen-nay
>
> Salsa

Ko'hoł Leyadidun'ona A:łashshi A:wan A:łashshina:we A:beyekkowa Bena:we
>
> **kgo**—holth / lay-ah-dee-**dune**-own-ah / **ahhh**-lthash-she / **ahhh**-wahn /
> **ahhh**-lthash-she-nah-way / **ahhh**-bay-ko-ah / **ben**-ah-way
>
> Predictions The Elders Heard From Their Parents

The rules of grammar and spelling are still being written for the Zuni language. Every effort has been made to present to you the best written Zuni. In time our written language will continue to develop and change just as English has and does. Meanwhile, we hope you enjoy your introduction to our language.

EDWARD WEMYTEWA
Pueblo of Zuni

Edward Wemytewa is the director of the Zuni Rainbow Project and founder of Idiwanan An Chawe (Children of the Middle Place), the first Zuni language theater company.

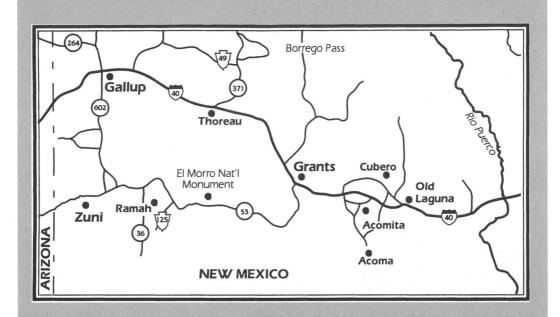

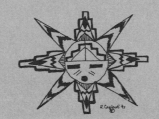

A WOMAN CARRYING LOAVES OF BREAD TO A BEEHIVE OVEN FOR BAKING. COURTESY OF ZUNI TRIBAL ARCHIVES.

IDONAPSHE
Let's Eat
TRADITIONAL ZUNI FOODS

Two women removing baked loaves of bread from a traditional beehive oven. Courtesy of the Smithsonian Institution.

Bread and Grains

HEBOK'O:MUWE
Sourdough Bread

KWIK'YA:MUWE
Milk Bread

DOWHEWE
Piki Bread

CHU:ᴌUPTS'INNA MU'LE CHIKWA
Yellow Cornmeal Sweet Bread

HEBATCHI:WE
Tortillas

HE:YAHONI:WE
Blue Corn Pancakes

MUKK'YALI:WE
Blue Corn Marbles

MUK'YABA:WE
Blue Cornmeal Patties

MUTS'IK'O:WE
Fry Bread or Turnovers

Hebok'o: Muwasha:we
BREAD MAKING

Talking and getting together while sourdough bread is being prepared is a part of clan activities. Usually the clan sisters will come to bake bread for an individual niece or nephew, either for a day's help or the full four days of a special event. This brings family relatives together to share news of the family's additions like a new baby or newlyweds and things that have happened in the family that everyone doesn't know about.

Sha'lak'o time (December) is when most of the families get together and help the family make sourdough bread. Making sourdough bread requires a lot of muscle work. Mixing three sacks of flour by yourself means you need a lot of help. The best part is when the bread comes out just perfect and all that work you did was worth it.

Ko'leho⧸ Hebok'o: Mulobe:n'ona
USING AN OUTDOOR OVEN TO BAKE BREAD

Build the fire at the outside oven while waiting for the dough to rise the first time.

While waiting for the dough to rise, put more wood in the oven until it is white inside.

After the fire is out, clean out the ashes in the oven with juniper branches. Dip the branches in water and dab them on the floor of the oven. If the water drops boil and evaporate, the oven is ready.

If the water doesn't boil, use wheat bran to test oven readiness.

Test the oven with wheat bran by scattering bran inside the oven. When the bran is golden brown, that's when you know that the bread is ready to be put in for baking.

If the bran burns, clean out the burned bran. Dip the branches in water and dab the floor of the oven to lower the temperature.

Two women and a child plastering a traditional beehive oven near the former Zuni farming village of Hawikkuh. Hawikkuh was the site of the first contact between Native Americans of the Southwest and the Spanish in 1539. Courtesy of the Museum of the American Indian. Photo by Jesse L. Nusbaum.

Hebok'o:muwe
SOURDOUGH BREAD

MAKES ABOUT 22 LOAVES (see below for small quantity baking)
Sourdough starter—about 8 cups made the night before the bread is
    to be baked (see recipe on p. 87.)
25 pounds flour
½ cup salt
1 package dry yeast
3 pounds lard

Using an outdoor oven: See directions for using an outdoor oven, called a beehive oven in Zuni, on page 4.

THE BREAD

Thoroughly mix the dry ingredients with your hands, adding water until all the flour is mixed and a little dry or hard. Add the lard. Start kneading until you can smell the sour smell. Cover the dough with a cloth and place in a warm spot. Let the dough rise to double its size. Build the fire in the outside oven.

Now start rolling out the dough to about the size of a baseball or a little bigger. After all the dough is rolled out, shape the dough into fancy or regular loaves. After all the dough is shaped, wait for it to rise a second time. Check your oven and add wood as necessary.

Place bread in ready oven and bake for about 45 minutes to about an hour. Bread should be done when it's golden brown. Then it is ready to eat.

USING A CONVENTIONAL OVEN AND BAKING FEWER LOAVES

1 cup starter	1 teaspoon yeast
5 pounds flour	¾ cup lard
1 teaspoon salt	

Mix as above. Place in bread pans. Place in 350 degree F oven for 30 minutes and then bake at 400 degrees F until brown. Makes 5 or 6 loaves.

Kwik'ya:muwe

MILK BREAD

15 LOAVES (12 INCHES ROUND). 1–2 SLICES PER SERVING
½ sack flour (12–15 pounds)
10 tablespoons baking powder
4 cups evaporated or reconstituted dried milk
2 teaspoons salt
1 pound lard
10 cups water (1½ cups of water for every 5 pounds of flour)

BEFORE MIXING, BUILD A FIRE in the outdoor oven. (See page 4 for using an outdoor oven.) If you are using a conventional oven, preheat to 350 degrees F.

Mix half a sack of flour and 10 tablespoons of baking powder. Add the milk and salt to the dry ingredients. Add the lard to mixture until small pea-size lumps of lard are formed. Start mixing in water until it's the consistency of soft dough.

After all your dough is mixed, roll it into balls about baseball size. Then flatten your dough to about half an inch and 6–8 inches in diameter. Put in fancy edging by pinching the edges as you would with a pie crust.

To make a glossy finish to your bread, pierce the top in 5 or 6 places and brush canned evaporated milk on the top before placing in the oven.

Check the outdoor oven to see if the oven is all white inside. When it is ready, put the bread in and check it in about 30 minutes. It is done when it's golden brown. The loaf will be about 2 inches high and should be sliced down the middle and then into 12–14 slices.

This bread also can be baked in a conventional oven at 350 degrees F until golden brown, approximately 45 minutes to one hour.

A:luwe
ZUNI FOOD COLORING
(LIMESTONE)

This form of food coloring is to make a blue color. This powder comes from white rocks. How it is done is to make a powder by burning manure with the rocks. When the manure burns down, the rocks are cooked. You must be careful when you pick up the rocks. Use a spoon to put them in the bowl. Sprinkle them with water and cover with a cloth and leave over night.

Check to make sure the rocks have turned to powder. If not all the rocks have turned into a powder, just take out those that didn't. If you want, you can burn them again or just throw them away.

Sift it to a fine powder. The powder can be stored for a long time.

To use as a food coloring, make it into a liquid form. Don't use all the powder to make the liquid. You will just need about 1 teaspoon of powder for 1 cup of water. Store the rest of the liquid in a screw-top jar and use as needed. You will need to replace the liquid when it loses its color. Use only a few drops until you can see the blue coloring on whatever you are making, whether it's dough or gravy.

Piki Stones

A slab of sandstone is treated with pumpkin seeds and the sap of cedar trees to make a piki stone. It is important that the person preparing the stone do it properly to ensure a good stone. This means working alone and concentrating on the stone.

Dowhewe
PIKI BREAD

20–25 SERVINGS, I ROLL PER PERSON
8 cups ground blue cornmeal, plus I cup for making initial batter.
1½ gallons water
½ teaspoon Zuni food coloring. (See p. 8)
1–4 inch pieces of sheep spinal cord or cow brain. A very light
    coating of lard or vegetable shortening can be substituted.

Build a fire under your piki stone.

MIXING THE GRAVY:

Sift the blue cornmeal. You will be making a soupy mixture of some of the blue cornmeal. Boil 1½ gallons of water in a pot. Make a paste of 1 cup cornmeal and ½ cup of water or more to get the consistency of gravy. Place the paste in a dipper (ladle) and put it in the boiling water spoonful by spoonful. Keep stirring to prevent scorching. The mix will get thicker as it boils.

MIXING THE DOUGH:

After that is done, put all your 8 cups blue cornmeal in a big mixing bowl and mix with warm water until dough is soft. Add about half a teaspoon of food coloring or less until you see the blue color in the dough.

When the stone is hot put a little bit of the cord or brain on a piece of cloth and rub the stone, to prevent sticking. Make a well in the cornmeal to the side of your bowl. Take a handful of the gravy mix and put it into the well and mix a thin batter of equal amounts of the gravy mixture and the dough mixture. (The blue cornmeal wall of your well forms a barrier to prevent the liquid from spreading while you are mixing the two elements.) Now grab a handful of the batter and spread it over the stone until your stone is all covered. Just wait until it starts to peel, then grab the edges and pull it off. Lay it on a piece of cloth. Repeat until all your dough and gravy is gone. When they have cooled, roll each sheet up. To keep them fresh you can roll them in plastic wrap.

Your hand may get very hot, so keep a bucket of water at your side to cool it off.

▲▼▲▼▲▼▲▼▲▼▲▼▲▼▲▼▲▼▲▼▲▼▲▼▲▼▲▼▲▼▲▼▲▼▲▼

Chu:ɬupts'inna Mu'le Chikwa
YELLOW CORNMEAL SWEET BREAD

SERVES 8–10
2 cups yellow cornmeal
½ cup white flour
½ cup sugar (or more to your taste)
3 teaspoons baking powder
½ cup milk
1 egg
½ cup warm water or more as needed to get the consistency of
    cake batter

MIX THE DRY INGREDIENTS IN A LARGE BOWL. Add one beaten egg and pour in the milk. Add the warm water a little at a time until it is like a cake batter. Pour the batter into a cake pan. Bake at 350 degrees F for about 30 minutes. When checking to see if it is done, use a toothpick. If inserted toothpick comes out clean, the cake is done.

You can eat this cake plain with beans or stew. If you would like to serve it as a dessert, add a fruit topping or frosting.

CHILDREN PLAYING NEAR BEEHIVE OVENS IN FRONT OF ZUNI PUEBLO WHEN IT
WAS SIX STORIES HIGH. COURTESY OF THE SMITHSONIAN INSTITUTION.

Hebatchi:we

TORTILLAS

10 TO 12 TORTILLAS
6 cups flour
4 teaspoons baking powder
1 teaspoon salt
½ cup dry milk
1 cup lard*
1 cup water, or more as needed

MIX FLOUR IN A LARGE BOWL along with baking powder, salt, dry milk, and lard. Mix ingredients thoroughly. Add water and mix until dough is not sticky but dry. Knead dough until it turns into a firm ball.

Pull dough into pieces the size of a golf ball for 6–8″ diameter tortillas or a tennis ball for 8–10″ diameter tortillas. After all the dough is made into balls flatten them out into thin ⅛″ circles. Put a griddle on the stove and turn the burner on medium high. Lightly grease the griddle and place the dough on the griddle. When the first side turns brown, flip the tortilla over and wait for the other side to brown. Unless you make a double batch, you should not need to grease the griddle again.

Stack your cooked tortillas on top of each other and wrap in a towel to keep them warm or place in a tortilla warmer.

*Using solid shortening: If you choose to use vegetable shortening you need to know that it does not brown the tortillas the way lard does. To prevent the yellowing that happens with vegetable shortening, delete the ½ dry milk and 1 cup water and add 1 cup liquid milk (at least 2% for some fat.)

He:yahoni:we
BLUE CORN PANCAKES

8 TO 10 PANCAKES
2 cups ground blue cornmeal
½ cup white flour
½ teaspoon salt
1½ teaspoons baking powder
½ cup evaporated milk or reconstituted dry milk
1 cup water—add more if needed

THOROUGHLY MIX DRY INGREDIENTS. Pour in milk and water until the batter is a smooth thin mixture. Heat your griddle to 350 degrees F. Pour your mixture to about 6 inches in diameter. Turn over each pancake when golden brown to cook the other side.

Serve with syrup, honey, or jam, or they can be eaten as a bread.

A LITTLE BOY IN FRONT OF ZUNI PUEBLO. COURTESY OF THE SMITHSONIAN INSTITUTION.

Mukk'yali:we

BLUE CORN MARBLES

SERVES 5–6
4 cups ground blue cornmeal
2 quarts water (set aside 1 cup for mixing the dough)
½–1 teaspoon Zuni food coloring (see page 8 for recipe)

BLUE CORNMEAL IS READY TO USE—it's roasted and ground really fine. Boil the water in a large pot. As the water is boiling, put the cornmeal in a medium-size bowl. After the water has boiled, extract 1 cup boiling water and pour into the mixture a little at a time until you get a soft dough. Stir with a spoon as the dough cools off. Knead the dough until the blue cornmeal flour is mixed. As you're kneading, pour in a dab of Indian food coloring. To achieve the consistency of bread dough, add water or flour as needed.

When all is mixed, start cutting small pieces of the dough to about the size of marbles. After all the dough is cut up put the marbles in the boiling water. Stir and let the mixture boil until it thickens. Boiling will make a gravy with corn marbles.

Blue Corn Marbles are used as a side dish for steaks, green tomatoes, or salsa. This meal is eaten during the winter time and can be eaten in the early spring. There is a saying that if you make Blue Corn Marbles during the summer and if its raining, it will hail. That's if it is raining.

Muk'yaba:we
BLUE CORNMEAL PATTIES

SERVES 8-10
4 cups of dried blue corn
1 teaspoon Zuni blue food coloring (see page 8 for recipe)
1½ cups warm water—for mixing
1 quart water—for boiling

GRIND DRIED BLUE CORN UNTIL COARSE, then pour into a medium size bowl. Pour in the warm water, along with the food coloring, into the ground blue corn. Knead the dough until all is mixed. Cut off small pieces of dough and shape into small balls. Flatten balls out to about 2 inches diameter, but not too thin, about ¼″ thick.

Boil the water in a large pot. Put in the patties and let boil for about 15 to 20 minutes. Stir carefully so the patties won't break. As they boil, the patties also make gravy which can be eaten along with the patties, or not, as you choose. Blue cornmeal patties are eaten at breakfast and are often served with bacon, eggs, and fried potatoes.

Muts'ik'o:we

FRY BREAD OR TURNOVERS

10–12 PIECES
4 cups flour
4 teaspoons baking powder
1 teaspoon salt
⅓ cup milk
1 cup water
1½ pounds lard (for frying, you can also use cooking oil)

THOROUGHLY MIX DRY INGREDIENTS TOGETHER. Add milk. Add water sparingly until dough is pliable or soft—to the point where it does not stick to your hands. If sticky, add flour instead—do not add any more water. Allow dough to rise about 5 minutes.

In a frying pan, or deep pot, heat oil to frying temperature. Roll your dough into small balls about the size of a tennis ball. Pat or roll your dough into thin round pieces. Drop the rolled dough into the hot oil or, to protect yourself from hot oil splatters, place dough in oil using a slotted spoon. Wait for one side to get golden brown, then flip the bread over with a long-handled fork or tongs. Once golden brown, lift bread out and place on paper towel to drain. Repeat until all is done.

A young girl carrying water for her traditional waffle garden
in an olla jar on her head. Courtesy of the Smithsonian Institution.

FRUITS AND VEGETABLES

TS'UPBACHI
Yucca Fruit Bananas

DUYA:WE
Prickly Pear Cactus

SHOTS'I'DO MILO:WE
Roast Sweet Corn

MIDALIK'O
Common Purslane

MO:DEYAŁA, MO:KISI, DAP ME:MO'LE
Dark Green, Grey-Green Striped, and Orange Pumpkin

MO:DEYAŁA
Fried Squash

ADO:WE/K'YAHE:WE
Wild Spinach

U'kwin Habo:li
YUCCA ROOT SHAMPOO

Yucca roots can be gathered when there is a need for their use. The roots will be cleaned by taking the bark off, chopping them into small pieces, and soaking them for awhile. When ready to use, add hot water. Swish your hands in the water till there are suds. Then you take out the roots. Start washing your hair. It's best to use the old roots because the young roots can sometimes cause itching and dryness.

Yucca roots can be used in many ways:

for funeral rites and other religious purposes,

as medicine men headpieces,

woven into donuts to carry pottery on your head,

in varnish for men's uses

as pottery brushes,

cut into strips for tying hot tamales,

to restore natural turquoise.

Bep'e
INDIAN HAIR BRUSH

Hair brushes can be made from alkali sacaton grass, which can be bundled. These brushes were used before modern hairbrushes were introduced. These brushes are still in use when there is corn grinding taking place. The ladies use the brushes to clean off the grinding stones.

This brush is very good at brushing out long hair. There is a hair piece which is made out of a willow stick. This is made to hold hair in place while a yarn is being tied to the hair. When the hair is tied, the hair piece is pulled out and now the hair is secure.

Ts'upbachi
YUCCA FRUIT BANANAS

1 BANANA PER PERSON TO BE SERVED,
APPROXIMATELY ¾ CUP PER PERSON
Yucca fruit bananas

YUCCA FRUIT IS PICKED AROUND SEPTEMBER OR OCTOBER when the fruit is reddish yellow.

Yucca fruit is washed, peeled, and put to boil in a large pot till it turns dark brown. Taken off the fire when it cools down, it is kneaded into logs or rolls.

Yucca fruit is used in many ways: medicine men use it for medicine purposes; it can be used for mixing paint for pottery, but using a lot will burn off the paint when fired; some cooks use it in pastries and jam; fruit rolls can be made and stored in tight covered containers for winter uses; cooked yucca fruit can be hung outside to dry on a line. After drying, it can be stored in cloth flour sacks and hung on the wall for winter and eaten as a snack.

A WOMAN AND A MAN COLLECTING PEACHES. A LOW-GROWING PEACH TREE WAS CULTIVATED BY ZUNI FARMERS TO GROW SUCCESSSFULLY IN ZUNI'S HIGH DESERT CLIMATE. COURTESY OF THE SMITHSONIAN INSTITUTION.

Duya:we
PRICKLY PEAR CACTUS FRUIT

SERVING DEPENDS ON HOW MUCH YOU PICK
Prickly pears

During late summer, August through September, prickly pear cactus flowers should be in bloom. When fruit is produced in September and October people take a basket and walk out to the mountains in search of cactus fruit. People use tongs to pick the fruit. After picking the fruit, they use juniper branches to brush off the stickers and roll the fruit around in the sand to remove the rest of the stickers. They bring the fruit home, clean it, and eat the fruit as it is.

One thing, do not eat the seeds! They cause constipation.

The pulp of the fruit can also be used to make a juice. Blend the pulp with water to make a sweet drink.

Prickly pear fruits are often available in markets in November and December, especially at those stores serving Hispanic communities. They may be called Nopales, a Spanish word.

Mo:chikwa Danay'a
PEACH ORCHARD

When I was little and my mother was still strong, I was twelve years old then. Behind Dowa Yalanne we had peach orchard trees (that) were producing a lot of peaches. We used to go watch the orchard. My mother and I would take our lunch and go to the spring and up the path to where the our orchard was. We used to stay all day. Toward the evening my mother would go and fill up a flour sack of peaches and I would carry some in my bucket and then we'd be off for home.

—Margaret Edaakie

Ko'leho͏́ Mobiya: A:k'usk'yanakya dap Ko'leho͏́ Akkya Ido:wo'e:n'ona
HOW TO DRY FRUIT AND USE IT IN COOKING

When there are plenty of ripe peaches, cut them in half and sun dry them on boards or on a cloth until they are all dried thoroughly. The dried pieces should be stored in cloth bags so that moisture won't develop. Dried peaches can be eaten dry, boiled until tender, or made into peach turnovers with brown sugar.

Apples can be dried in the same way as the peaches get dried. They can be boiled with sugar for pies.

When there are a lot of ripe melons, they can be cut into strips, put on boards to dry or be hung up like chile ristras. When dry, put in a cloth bag to keep dry. They can be eaten as is, or the melon can be moistened for tenderness.

Shots'i'do Milo:we
ROAST SWEET CORN

FOR LARGE GROUPS OF PEOPLE
corn   1 ear for each person to be served
water   as much as needed to wet the corn

SWEET CORN CAN BE ROASTED IN THE OUTDOOR OVEN. You need about one fourth of pick-up truck load or five gunny sacks for a small outdoor oven. Note: the oven needs to be filled with corn or else the corn will burn. Build the fire day or night. When the oven is hot and white inside with a lot of hot charcoal, it is ready. Sprinkle water on the corn. When you get the corn inside the oven it will produce moisture. Cover the front and top openings of the oven with a rock slab. Plaster over the slabs with a mud mixture to seal all openings.

Roast the corn for about 12 hours. They are ready to eat.

You can also roast corn on hot charcoals. Keep turning your corn while it is cooking to prevent burning. Be sure you have just charcoal and no burning wood, otherwise your corn will be smoky. When the corn is done, wipe clean before eating.

FOR STORING "JUST OUT OF THE OVEN" CORN:
Take your corn out of the oven and spread it on a canvas until all the corn is out of the oven. Take the corn by the husks and string them up to dry. When you are ready for corn, you just reboil it. There's your fresh sweet corn.

Dried sweet corn can be ground to a meal and made into soup. Roast corn can be shared with families and neighbors. The kernels can be removed from the cob and used in soup dishes.

Deshkwi is a time of fasting for Zunis and no animal fats are eaten during this time. Dried corn can be used to make a good Deshkwi meal. Dried corn can be boiled with beans for a delicious meal.

Miwe dap A:wan Haydoshna:we
CORN AND ITS USES

In Zuni, corn crops come in different colors such as white, blue, yellow, red, black and speckled. Sweet corn Shots'i'do, trail corn, Mi'l onap'ona, and popcorn, Dak'una:we are some of the different kinds of corn grown in Zuni.

The Kachinas use the corn colors in their religious ceremonies and the directions also use the colors of the corn. For the North the color is yellow and is called Bishlankwi. The South's color is red which is called Ma'k'yayakwi. The East is white and called Dewankwi. The West is blue and called Sunha:kwi. Up is multi-colored and is called I:yamakwi. Down or nadir is black and is called Manikkyakwi.

Corn is ground into a meal which is used for praying and preparing foods like hot tamales, cornmeal soup, corn bread, and posole. Mostly white corn is used in all our cooking.

Usually blue corn is used for our traditional cooking. Blue corn is sometimes used for raw cooking. (Blue corn can be ground without being toasted.)

Corn is used to test girls who are just reaching puberty.

When a girl is getting herself into marriage, there is a test involving corn. In the traditional way, a girl is tested to see how well she can do the work required, such as corn grinding. Her success will be seen by the young man's family and they will decide whether or not she is accepted. So, she will be asked to fix a meal of the young man's family's choice with cornmeal she has ground.

Midalik'o
COMMON PURSLANE
PORTULACACEAE

SERVES 6–8
4 cups of midalik'o
1 ½ cups ground white cornmeal
½ cup water or more as necessary to make cornmeal paste
8 cups of water for boiling
¼ cup chile if desired

SINCE ITS BEEN RAINING THIS YEAR (1997), we should have good midalik'o. It grows on the ground and it spreads out wide. Midalik'o should be harvested in early June while it is still green and before it has flowered.

First you pick and wash the midalik'o. If there has been bread baking, you can put it in the oven and toast it. If you picked a lot, it can be saved for another meal. Boil the midalik'o in a medium-size pot with water. When it boils, make a paste of the white cornmeal and ½ cup water. Add paste until the mixture thickens like a soup. You can add chiles here if desired. Let it simmer for 10 minutes and it's ready to eat.

Midalik'o is delicious before your main course or is a good side dish with meat.

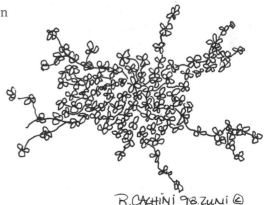

R.CACHINI 98.ZUNI ©

A WOMAN AND A CHILD IN FRONT OF AN ADOBE HOME. PUMPKINS ARE
GROWING IN TRENCH GARDENS. COURTESY OF THE SMITHSONIAN
INSTITUTION.

Mo:deyaƚa, Mo:k'isi, dap Me:mo'le
DARK GREEN, GREY-GREEN STRIPED,
AND ORANGE PUMPKINS

SERVES 30 OR MORE
1 pumpkin

ORANGE PUMPKINS CAN BE KEPT FOR A SHORT TIME, usually one month. Greenish grey pumpkins can be kept for a longer time. These two pumpkins can be cooked in outdoor or conventional ovens, or can be cut and boiled over the stove. After cooking it, pumpkin can be used in making pies.

BAKED PUMPKIN

Place the pumpkin whole in a cake pan and cover with foil. If cooking in a conventional oven bake at 350 degrees F until tender. Check after 45 minutes by piercing with a fork. If the pumpkin is tender and smells good, it's cooked. If baking in an outdoor oven with pots of stew, your pumpkin will stay in the oven overnight. Butter, honey, or sugar can be added as a sweetener to baked pumpkin when serving.

ROASTED PUMPKIN SEEDS

Clean the pumpkin flesh off the seeds. Spread the seeds on a lightly greased cookie sheet and place in the oven at 250 degrees F for about an hour, turning occasionally. You can add salt, chile powder, or other spices to seeds while they are roasting.

As I can remember, they used to can pumpkins and vegetables at Nutria. People that were in home economic groups from Blackrock (in Zuni) used to go out to farming places when it was harvesting time and they helped the village people in canning.

Mo:deya'la
FRIED SQUASH

6 1½-CUP SERVINGS
8 cups squash—zucchini, patty pan, or gooseneck (crookneck)
    are good varieties to use
4 tablespoons oil

THERE ARE ABOUT THREE DIFFERENT TYPES OF SQUASH that can be fried. They are zucchini, patty pan, and gooseneck. All these squash can be cut and frozen for winter uses.

Peel squash if necessary or desired. Slice the squash and heat oil in frying pan on medium heat. You can bread your cut pieces and then fry them, or fry them plain. Try adding sliced green chile, onion, and bacon while frying to make it tasty.

Hek'yats'otda: Oneya:wakkya K'yahelleyanne
USE RUSTY NAILS TO FIX WILD SPINACH

Boil the spinach in a big pot. Put in rusty nails or rusty things. You could also toast a corn (on the cob), scrape it, and put it in whole. This will give (the spinach) a toasty taste.

—Lolita Edaakie

Ado:we *(before cooking)*
K'yahe:we *(after cooking)*
WILD SPINACH
(ROCKY MOUNTAIN BEE PLANT)

10 INDIVIDUAL STALKS, AFTER COOKING, WILL YIELD 2 CUPS. SERVES 5.

10   stalks (The wild spinach is picked before the plant flowers. You
       will cook only the leaves and the side stems, not the main stalk.)
2   gallons water
2–3 rusty nails, 1 old horseshoe, or 1 dried toasted corn cob

WILD SPINACH IS PICKED IN THE EARLY SUMMER when it is still fresh and tender. A plant should not be cut a lot, so it will grow some more.

After cutting all the spinach you want, take it home. Take the leaves and stems and wash them. In a big pot boil the spinach in lots of water to get the bitter taste out. Cooking lots of spinach at once also helps to remove the bitter taste. Some people put a dry toasted corn cob with the kernels still on it in the boiling water, while some others use rusty nails to help get the bitter taste out faster. After it is cooked, the spinach is shared among the family members. It can be eaten as a side dish for meat.

To cook a large quantity, gather two gunny sacks with about 60–70 stalks in each sack and cook in 10 gallons of water.

View over the rooftops of Zuni Pueblo looking southeast toward Dowa Yalanne (Corn Mountain). The Zuni River is seen just beyond the pueblo. Courtesy of the Smithsonian Institution.

Soups and Stews

WA:KESHI TSULEYANNE
Beef Stomach Stew

KYANE:LU TSULEYANNE
Sheep Stomach Soup

CHULEYA:WE
Posole Stew

K'YAWAHO:WE
Chile Stew

OKSHIK SUMAPBONNE
Rabbit Stew

NA'LE SHIK'USNA: DAP K'YABIMOWE WOLEYANNE
Deer Jerky Soup

METDA: WOLEYANNE
Prickly Pear Cactus Soup

NOLEYA:WE
Pinto Bean Soup

OHE: WOLEYANNE
Squash Seed Soup

HEKKWIDOLA
Fresh Corn Smut Soup

CHUWE SUMAPBONNE
White Corn Soup or Mush

HEKK'I:WE
Blue Corn Soup

Wa:kyashi Tsuleyanne
BEEF STOMACH STEW—TRIPE

SERVES 10–12 FROM APPROXIMATELY ⅙ OF THE STOMACH
8 cups tripe
1 cup frozen white posole corn
1½ gallons water
1½ cups of chile paste—red or green (see page 82 for recipe)

THE STOMACH OF THE COW IS CLEANED by taking off the sponge-like stomach lining. Cut up the stomach into meal-size pieces of 12 inches by 12 inches. You will use one big piece to make stew. The remaining pieces can either be frozen or dried for later use.

Fill a stock pot with water. Cut the tripe into pieces. Boil the tripe and white posole corn until tender or when the posole has popped open. As the water boils it evaporates and the cooking corn absorbs water, so add more water as needed. Add chile paste and there's your meal.

Kyane:lu Tsuleyanne
SHEEP STOMACH SOUP

SERVES 15
sheep stomach (tripe)
1½ gallons water
1 teaspoon salt
chile paste (see page 82 for recipe)

CLEAN OUT THE STOMACH REALLY WELL, being sure to clean out all the folds in the stomach. Cut the stomach into small pieces about 2 inches square. Put water in a large pot with salt and bring to a boil. Add the stomach pieces and boil until tender and the water has simmered to the consistency of soup. Cooking time will be approximately 2 to 3 hours depending on how much stomach is cooked at one time. Serve with chile paste.

Generally this soup is served as a meal by itself or with sourdough bread.

Chuleya:we
POSOLE STEW

SERVES 15, 2 CUP SERVING SIZE
1 pound dry white corn for posole*
2 pounds stew meat, cubed (beef or mutton)
1 pound meat bones
1 teaspoon salt
2 gallons water (more may need to be added as stew cooks)
*If your family prefers more corn than meat in their stew, try using 2
    pounds of posole.*

PREPARING THE POSOLE:

The night or the day before making your stew, prepare the white corn. In warm water, soak the corn in a bowl for 3–5 minutes. Test the corn with your finger to see if you can easily peel off the outer shell. If so, drain the water and put the corn on the grinding stone and start rolling the corn until the outer layer of the corn starts to peel off. Sift the corn clean. Use a willow basket to sift your corn clean or you can use a colander.

Short-cut: purchase a 1 pound package of frozen posole and follow directions to prepare.

PREPARING THE STEW:

To make the stew, cut the meat into bite-size pieces. Boil the water in a stock pot or other large pot. Put your meat, bones, and prepared corn in the boiling water. Add a little bit of salt so that it won't boil over. The way you can tell if it's ready is when the corn looks like popcorn. Posole stew goes good with chile.

DON'T HAVE A GRINDING STONE IN YOUR KITCHEN?

You can use an unpainted, rough-surfaced patio tile as a substitute. Be sure you clean the stone before using. Also, soaking the stone before using will prevent you from picking up a lot of grit from the rock while rolling and grinding.

Kya𝘭𝘭ada:we

BUTCHERING SHEEP

First you would need to buy a sheep to butcher. Cut the neck and let all the blood drain. The blood is saved for stuffing stomach sausage. The blood is stirred regularly to prevent it setting up like gelatin. Then you start skinning the sheep with a sharp knife. You need to be careful not to cut off the meat.

When you are all done skinning, open the abdomen. There are two layers of lining, so be careful not to cut the stomach. Cut open the neck to take out the esophagus. Separate and tie the red colored esophagus, so the waste won't drain out, and remove the esophagus with the lungs and liver. Again, you will need to tie the intestine connected to the esophagus so as not to drain the waste.

Take out the stomach and the intestines, leaving the kidneys. Clean out the blood left behind. Clean the stomach, washing the intestines and stomach with plain, warm water. Cut off the head and hoofs and singe them over hot charcoal, then wash off the singed wool. Cook the head and hoofs together in the oven in a large pot of water to cure the pieces. No part of the sheep is wasted, and many different meals can come from one sheep.

Long time ago store traders used to buy sheep pelts. They would weigh the pelt and you would get a dime or a quarter for it.

A sheepherder's hut northwest of Dowa Yalanne. Courtesy of the Smithsonian Institution.

Kyane:lu Wowilli: Benawe
SHEEP HERDING STORIES

As I was growing up I used to stay with my parents at sheep camp. My parents would get up in the morning together and go to take the sheep out of the sheep pens and let them roam around to eat. A sheepherder's work was hard work, but the times that I liked were the lambing times and sheep shearing times. At lambing times the little lambs were so playful. Sheep shearing times were when you could sell sheep skin and wool if you were not lazy. You could make some extra money by doing this.

The food that we usually ate at sheep camp was beans, potatoes, canned and dried food. Once in a great while a sheep was butchered to eat and the best treat I liked was sheep tails. The tails got singed and washed. After it was boiled the tail could be eaten as a meal with chile paste. The rest of the meat was made into jerky because there was no refrigerator. Only kerosene lamps were used. Summertime outdoor cooking was fun.

K'yawaho:we
CHILE STEW, WITH OR WITHOUT POTATOES

SERVES 6–7

With Potatoes
2 pounds stew meat (your choice)
2 tablespoons oil
8 cups water
6–8 peeled, diced potatoes

Without Potatoes
2 pounds stew meat
2 tablespoons oil
8 cups water
½ cup flour
1 tablespoon cornstarch

CHILE PASTE
2 cups red chile
1–2 cloves garlic
2 tablespoons dried cilantro seeds or ½ cup chopped fresh cilantro
1 cup water, or more if needed

WITH POTATOES:
Cut meat into bite-size pieces and brown in a large pot in oil. Add water, and cook to boiling over medium heat. Blend chile, garlic, cilantro, and water to make chile paste. When the meat and water start to boil, put in your chile paste. Stir regularly to prevent lumping. While the mixture is boiling, prepare your potatoes and put them in the pot with your boiling meat and chile. Stew will be ready when the potatoes are tender.

WITHOUT POTATOES:
Cut meat into bite-size pieces and brown in a large pot in oil. Add water, and cook to boiling over medium heat. Blend chile, garlic, cilantro, and water for the chile paste. When the meat and water start to boil put in your chile paste, flour, and cornstarch. Stir regularly to prevent lumping. The stew will thicken as it boils and be ready in about 10 or 15 minutes or when meat is tender.

Okshik Sumapbonne
RABBIT STEW

SERVES 6–8
1 rabbit (1½—2 pounds of meat)
1 tablespoon of oil
enough water to cover rabbit plus two inches
1 cup dry white corn or ½ cup ground cornmeal
salt, if desired
chile paste, if desired (see page 82 for recipe)

RABBIT STEW IS A GREAT MEAL. Skin the rabbit and clean out the intestines. Cut the rabbit up into parts and wash it.

Brown the meat in oil. Put water in a large pot and bring it to a boil. Add browned rabbit and boil it for about 30 minutes or until tender. As the rabbit is boiling, grind white corn into a coarse meal. Then put the ground cornmeal in the boiling water until it thickens and becomes the consistency of gravy. Chile paste can be added to your taste. Enjoy.

Na'le Shik'usna:
dap K'yabimowe Woleyanne
DEER JERKY SOUP

10–12 BOWLS
2 cups deer jerky*
2 tablespoons cooking oil
4 cups diced potatoes
8 cups water

POUND THE DRY DEER JERKY into bite-size pieces and brown in cooking oil. Boil water in a large pot. Add prepared jerky to water and boil for 15 to 20 minutes or until tender. Add the potatoes. You'll have a nice thick soup that is ready when the potatoes are tender. Serve with oven bread.

You can add any spices to the cooking soup to your personal taste such as salt, pepper, garlic, onion, or coriander.

*If you don't have any deer jerky, you can substitute beef jerky.

Metda: Woleyanne

PRICKLY PEAR CACTUS SOUP

SERVES 8 TO 10

6–7 large pieces of cactus pads
1 cup ground white corn (white cornmeal)
8 cups water (You will need to add more at boiling stage.)

First you have to find wide pieces of cactus. Pick them off with tongs and take off as many of the sharp stickers as you can by brushing them with juniper branches or other rough material to protect your hands.

When you have brought the cactus pieces home, place them in a cake pan and put in an oven at 350 degrees F. Toast the cactus on both sides to help burn off the rest of the stickers. Scrape off any burned material and wash the cactus. Cut the cactus into bite-size pieces. Boil until tender. Add ground white cornmeal to make a thick gravy. Boil down, about 20–30 minutes, so it is like a soup and it's ready to eat. Serve with bread and chile.

Prickly pear cactus is native to the Southwest. Cactus pads and the fruit are sometimes available in specialty grocery stores.

Two men using sticks to winnow white beans. Courtesy of the Smithsonian Institution.

Noleya:we
PINTO BEAN SOUP

SERVES 6–7
1 pound pinto beans
4 quarts water
½ pound bacon
1 teaspoon salt

WASH THE BEANS. Boil the water in a large pot and put in the beans. Cut up the bacon into bite-size pieces and put it in with the beans. Add salt. Add water as necessary to keep it like a soup. Let it cook on low for about four hours.

Test the beans and see if they are soft. If soft, the soup is ready to be served as a meal. You can add hot or mild chile paste or powder to taste.

Try the soup with fry bread (recipe on page 17) or a tortilla (recipe on page 12).

Adeya: Mu'le
SQUASH BLOSSOM FLOWER CAKE

(Recipe from Frances Wytsalucey as told to Rita Edaakie.)

Roast the blue corn. Grind the corn into a fine flour. Have the flowers cleaned and ready. She said they would have the flour in their mouth and wet it with their own saliva. She said it will produce a sweet taste. So what they chewed on will have to go into the flower pockets. Line them (the flowers) up depending on how much you want to make. Put them on top of a hot stove or on a hot griddle and brown. Turn over and brown on both sides. "If, she said, I were to make them (the cakes) as I explained (the directions), they (the young people) won't eat them."

Ohe: Woleyanne
SQUASH SEED STEW
(Recipe from Lolita Edaakie)

SERVES 6—8

4–6 cups of squash seeds (Lolita Edaakie likes to use striped grey
    pumpkin, but you can use butternut squash or any squash with
    large seeds.)

2 quarts water

1 cup white corn to grind for meal or ½ cup ground meal

BREAK OPEN A SQUASH, take out the seeds, and let them dry for awhile (indoors on aluminum foil or waxed paper). Then open the seeds and grind them coarse (in a cornmeal grinder). Toast the seeds in a pot and add water to let them boil (in a medium size pot). While waiting for the water to boil, grind white corn coarse and add it to the seeds and water a little at a time to thicken the broth. Now you have squash seed stew. Serve this stew with oven bread or tortillas. You may add any favorite spices to this stew.

Delakweyip Doye:nak'ya
SPRING PLANTING

Sho:do:ts'i is now about to plant his garden. He goes down to his field to give an offering. After the offering, he goes home and tells his grandmother to get ready (that is, to get the seeds ready for him). His grandmother puts the corn in the basket. She starts taking the kernels off the corn cobs. When she gets through she sifts the corn and gets the seeds of the fast-growing flowers hambassa, ohba:tsi, and Jamattsa/dowamattsa. She wets the flowers in a small bowl. With a prayer she rubs the corn with the flowers so the corn is ready to plant when Sho:do:ts'i says that it's time to set the corn in the fields. This is how the corn is prepared for planting.

Now it's time for prayers to help the seed grow. When the corn sprouts, it's really a blessing to see. If all the seeds are put in, the corn will mature and sprout. So much will come up and greet the sun. It is now the farmer who must greet the plants everyday until they mature and bear their children. When the corn is ready to come home and meet the ones of last year, again prayers are said in greeting and acceptance—the new corn meeting the old corn.

Now the corn is ripe. It is time to bring the corn home. At harvesting time, all the family will need to help in getting the corn off the cornstalks. When they come home, the grandmas will gather and take the cornhusks off for their own use. Cornhusks are used in a lot of different ways.

When you handle corn be careful with it. Don't put it in the trash, don't waste the corn. Dispose of it properly because it is one of our richest resources.

So now the family has fresh corn to eat. Corn for eating will always be available from roasted corn, sweet corn bread, and boiled corn or however you want to cook corn.

Traditional Zuni waffle gardens lining the north bank of the Zuni
River. Courtesy of the Museum of the American Indian.

Hekkwidola
FRESH CORN SMUT SOUP

SERVES 4–5
1 cup pumpkin seeds
1 corn smut, 6 or 7 inches long
6 cups water
2 cups white cornmeal

F RESH CORN SMUT IS A FUNGUS and located on the stalk where a cob would form. It develops during the early growth of the plant. It is a long, grey tube inside a husk, but unlike on a corn cob, the husk opens up as the smut grows. Use only when it has the texture and feel of a mushroom. It adds a sweet taste. When it has dried out and become a powder, do not use. Not every corn stalk has a corn smut. You can pick the smut off with your fingers.

Some families dry these by rolling them up in a cloth and tying the ends with string. The rolls are stored in a cool, dark place and are used in winter. If the smut is thick it should be cut to a ½ inch thickness before drying.

Once you've tasted it, you will be sure to ask for seconds.

DIRECTIONS
First the pumpkin seeds are toasted in a 350 degree F oven until brown. Put water in a medium pot and heat to boiling; add smut and pumpkin seeds when water is boiling. The smut breaks into pieces as it is boiled and the liquid has thickened. White cornmeal is added to make a soup. Serve with steak and chile.

Smut, ground into a powder, is sometimes used by Zuni men as a paint for their religious doings.

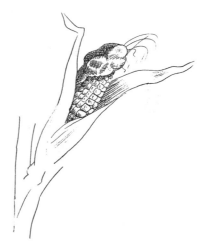

Chuwe Sumapbonne
WHITE CORN SOUP OR MUSH

SERVES 4 TO 6
1 pound stew meat, your choice
1 medium onion, chopped
1 tablespoon oil
1½ quarts water—for boiling
2 cups warm water
1½ cups white cornmeal or more (depending upon thickness desired)

CUT THE MEAT INTO BITE-SIZE PIECES. Brown the meat and chopped onion in oil. Put the meat and onion in a medium pot with water and let boil for about 15 minutes. Mix the cornmeal in a bowl with the 2 cups warm water until it looks like a thin mix. Pour the mix slowly into the pot of boiling water. Let the soup boil for 15 to 20 minutes, stirring constantly to prevent lumps and achieve desired thickness.

Make some tortillas and fix a plate of roasted green chiles to serve with your soup.

Hekk'iːwe

BLUE CORN SOUP

(OFTEN CALLED ATOLE, A SPANISH WORD, IN THE SOUTHWEST)

SERVES 6 TO 8 (1½ CUP SERVING SIZE)
10 cups water
1 cup ground blue cornmeal

IN A MEDIUM STEWING POT bring 10 cups of water to boil. In a bowl, mix the blue cornmeal with 1¾ cups of the warm water. Stir until it is like a pancake batter. Pour mixture in the boiling water. Using a whisk or spoon, keep stirring to prevent lumps and simmer over low heat for 5 minutes. It's ready when it is the consistency of soup. Pour in cups or bowls. Salt and sugar can be used if desired, or just eat "as is."

This meal is good for breakfast and goes well with eggs or steak. With a dash of salt it makes a good appetizer, and when sweetened with sugar or honey, it makes a great dessert. As a between-meal snack, the Zuni name for this dish is *yepnaːwe*.

Turkeys, chicks, and a puppy roaming through the pueblo. Courtesy of the Museum of the American Indian. Photo by George H. Pepper.

Main Dishes

CHUTS'IYA:MUWE
Blue Corn Tamales

K'YAYUMUWE
Fresh Sweet Corn Tamales

K'OLA MUWE
Hot Tamales

NI:SHA:BAK'O DAP K'UDEBAƚDO EYA
Doves and Ducks

DONA ALONNE
Roast Turkey

WA:KYASH AN K'ODOSSO:WE
Beef Intestines

KYANE:LU K'OPBOWA:WE
Sheep Intestines

K'USHI ALONNE
Prairie Dog Meal

CHUMMALI
Locusts with Cornmeal Mush

Chuts'iya:muwe
BLUE CORN TAMALES

10 –12 TAMALES
8 cups dried whole blue corn kernels that were cut from the cob
10 cups of wood ashes
water, enough for gravy consistency
2 bundles of corn husks (2 husks per tamale, plus 2 extra for strings)
1 gallon of water for boiling

SIFT THE BLUE CORN KERNELS to remove any debris. Sift the ashes to get the big charcoal and bits of twigs out. Place ashes in a large pot. Add enough water to the sifted ashes to create the consistency of gravy. Bring to a boil and add blue corn. Let it boil until the outer shell comes off the corn. When you see that the outer shell is coming off, remove from the heat. Wash corn with cold water until it is all clean.

Now grind the corn into a coarse meal. Clean the corn husks with warm water. Take one or two corn husks and tear ¼-inch wide strips length-wise. Now you are ready to make Blue Corn Tamales.

Divide the mush by the number of tamales you are making. Put the mush on the inside of one corn husk and cover the top with another corn husk. Tie with a husk string at each end about 1 inch in from the end. When all is done, boil the tamales for 10 to 15 minutes and they are ready to eat with posole stew and chile.

A Zuni man, woman, and child traveling on a road. Courtesy of the Smithsonian Institution.

K'yayumuwe

FRESH SWEET CORN TAMALES

5 OR 6 TAMALES
12 fresh corn-on-the-cob or 2 cans sweet corn
10 to 12 corn-husks (if using fresh corn, use husk from the corn)
1 gallon of water for boiling

TAKE THE CORN HUSK OFF THE CORN. Cut off the kernels off of the cob with a knife and put in a blender to make a paste. Put a tablespoon of corn mush on the inside of one corn-husk and cover the top with another corn-husk. Tie with a husk string at each end.

Place tamales in a pot of boiling water for 10 to 15 minutes.

These tamales can be served as a bread or vegetable side dish with soups and stews.

K'yayumuwe
FRESH CORN TAMALES

On Sunday I made some fresh corn tamales. The first thing I bought was some fresh corn from Stone Boot Guy (Stanley Gchachu.) It tasted sweet. I brought it home and started cutting off the kernels with a knife and I grinded the kernels on the hand grinder. I used the husks that was from the corn and put my grinded corn on the husks to make tamales. Then I boiled them and had one for myself. It was delicious.

— Vera Laweka

K'ola Muwe

HOT TAMALES

12–15 TAMALES
8 cups white corn
2 pounds of meat—pork or beef
1 onion, chopped
2 tablespoons of lard
4 cups of blue cornmeal for covering
1 bag of cornhusks (2 husks per tamale are needed)
2 quarts water
3 cups Chile Paste* (see page 82 for recipe)
If you are new to spicy foods, start with only 1½ cups of chile paste

GRIND THE WHITE CORN TO A COARSE MEAL. Cut up and brown the meat and chopped onion. After the meat is cooked, put the meat in a medium-size pot, and add water to about half-way, and add the chile paste. Let the meat, lard, and chile paste boil for a while.

Then put the white cornmeal *in a little at a time.* The mixture will thicken, so you have to watch out how much white cornmeal you put in. The consistency needs to allow you to form a small ball of mixture to place in your cornhusk, like a coarse cookie dough, but not too dry.

Now to clean the cornhusks. Rinse them out with warm water and wipe them clean. When that is done, put the blue cornmeal in a bowl and mix with warm water to a consistency of pancake batter.

To make a tamale, put a spoonful of blue cornmeal on a cornhusk and spread around with a spoon. On top of the blue cornmeal put a tablespoon of chile mush. Put more blue cornmeal covering the chile mush. Put a cornhusk over the ready made tamale. Strip a husk to make two ties to hold the cornhusk in place at each end.

After all the chile mush is used up, boil the tamales for 10 to 15 minutes.

These are wonderful when served with chuleya:we (posole stew.)

Two women collecting water in olla jars at the Zuni River.
Courtesy of the Museum of New Mexico (no. 37366). Photo by
H.F. Robinson.

Ni:sha:bak'o dap K'udebaɫdo Eya
DOVES AND DUCKS

1 DUCK (3½ TO 4½ POUNDS) SHOULD SERVE 3—4 PEOPLE
or 1 dove per person

DOVES AND DUCKS are prepared like all other wild birds. They need to be plucked, cleaned, and boiled to clean out the interior of the bird. Let the bird boil for an hour and let it cool off. Today it is possible to purchase these birds from a butcher or supermarket.

ROASTING DOVE
Preheat oven to 350 degrees F. Prepare the dove anyway you desire, perhaps brushing with some butter or maybe adding a little stuffing. Then put in a roaster and let it cook for about 25–30 minutes or until medium rare.

SLOW ROASTING DUCK
Preheat oven to 325 degrees F. Pierce the skin all over and place breast down in the roaster. Cook for 3 hours. Increase temperature to 350 degrees F and cook for 45 minutes.

Pick a favorite side dish such as corn or mashed potatoes and serve your meal.

Dowa Yalanne
Corn Mountain, Sacred Mountain

The elders used to tell us about the great flood when we were young. They told us that as the water was rushing in from all sides into the village, people started to panic. The people were told that the Corn Mountain was the only safe place to take refuge. The people took only what they could carry to the top of the mountain. Up on the mountain they took turns watching the water coming up the side of the mountain wall. People again started to panic at the rise of water coming up towards the Corn Mountain.

People gathered and talked of how they could be saved. They would have to sacrifice someone. One of the priests spoke. "I will give my daughter who is still a virgin." Another priest said "I will give my son who is also pure." The girl and boy were asked to come to a meeting that was being held, and that's where they were told that they had been given to the people to help stop the flood. The girl and boy accepted and were honored.

The men started getting prayer sticks ready while the ladies got clothes for the girl and boy to wear. They both took a bath with the ladies' help. When everything was ready they took the girl and the boy to the place where the prayer sticks were being prepared. When the prayer sticks were ready, these two were given the prayer sticks. People started a walkway to the edge and sprinkled cornmeal as the girl and boy went by. When they got to the edge the men got hold of them and lowered them into the water. Holding tight to the prayer sticks, the girl and boy disappeared into the water. People cried for the young ones sacrificing for the people. In doing this the girl and boy had set an example for the people.

Four days passed and the water stayed at the same level, but not coming up anymore. This was a time when four days meant four years. After four years the water ceased rising and stayed at the same level. Bubbles foamed on top. Around the mountain where you see the white rim is where the water was around this mountain and where the water rushed down and formed crevices. The people lived a long time on the Corn Mountain, hunting and planting to survive. Years and years passed until the people moved back down to where we live today. Those stone pillars that stand by Dowa Yalanne represent those young ones who gave up their lives to let our people live and prosper to who we are today.

Women who are having problems having babies go to the stone pillars to pray for maturity.

SOUTH-SOUTHWEST SIDE OF DOWA YALANNE. GALESTINA WASH IS IN THE FOREGROUND AND IT EMPTIES INTO THE ZUNI RIVER WHEN IT FLOWS. COURTESY OF ZUNI TRIBAL ARCHIVES.

Dona Alonne

ROAST TURKEY

20 SERVINGS
15 lb whole turkey, wild or domestic and fresh or thawed frozen
Stuffing:
4 stalks celery
1½ cups bread crumbs
2 onions
gizzards, chopped and cooked
1 stick butter, melted

RINSE THE TURKEY CLEAN. Cook and chop the gizzards. Prepare the stuffing by mixing the celery, bread crumbs, onion, and gizzards. Pour melted butter over the dressing and stir. Now stuff the turkey cavity. Close the turkey cavities with toothpicks. Put the turkey in the roaster to cook. Can be cooked in outdoor or conventional oven. It takes about four hours to cook. Wild turkeys cook faster than domestic turkeys. Check a wild turkey after three hours. When the turkey is done, fix side dishes, and there is your turkey dinner.

R. Cachini 97©

A MAN CARRYING A LOAD OF WOOD UP TO THE SECOND STORY OF THE
PUEBLO. OVENS WERE BUILT ON THE ROOFTOOPS OF EACH STORY AND COOK-
ING DONE ON EVERY LEVEL. COURTESY OF THE SMITHSONIAN INSTITUTION.

Wa:kyash An K'odosso:we
BEEF INTESTINES

SERVES 4–5
beef intestines

THE INTESTINES ARE WASHED, turned inside out and cut into 4–6 foot lengths. Tie each section at one end and blow air into the other end by the mouth. Then tie that end. See illustrations.

Hang the sections out to dry. Place sections you don't plan to use in a plastic bag and store in the freezer for later use. Dried sections will be approximately 6–8 inches long.

To cook, place dry intestines in a cake pan and bake in a 450 degree F oven until brown and crispy, about 30 minutes. Be sure and check them every 5–10 minutes to prevent burning them.

Sprinkle with salt and pepper to taste and they are ready to eat.

Serve with mashed potatoes, green beans, or corn.

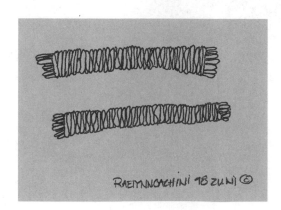

Kyane:lu K'opbowa:we
SHEEP INTESTINES

8–10 PIECES
Sheep intestines, from a freshly butchered sheep or purchased at the
market already prepared.

CLEAN OUT THE INTESTINES. Cut the ones that have fat on them 6 to 8 inches long.
Use those that are without fat to wrap or coil around the cut pieces. See illustration below. Note: Intestines purchased at the store will come already prepared.

Place wrapped intestines in a pan or casserole. Cook the intestines in a conventional oven at 350–375 degrees F until they brown, about 30 minutes.

Sheep intestines and Chile Stew go great together.

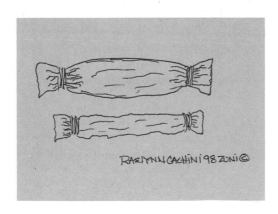

TWO MEN BUILDING A FENCE. COURTESY OF THE SMITHSONIAN INSTITUTION.

K'ushi Alonne

PRAIRIE DOG MEAL

SERVES 3-4
1 prairie dog (a squirrel can be substituted)
butter
salt
pepper

MAKING A PRAIRIE DOG DINNER is just like roasting a chicken. Once a prairie dog is killed it needs to be cleaned. Singe off the hair and clean the intestines inside and out.

Preheat the oven to 350 degrees F. Rub the carcass with butter and sprinkle with salt and pepper. Place a small cedar or juniper branch inside the stomach. Put the prairie dog in a roaster in the oven. It takes about 1 hour to cook. If the roast is brown, it's ready to eat.

Now that all their natural predators are gone, prairie dogs are more plentiful than they once were. It is always important when preparing and eating wild foods to be sure the plants and animals are healthy. Check with your local game authorities about the hunting and eating of local wild plants and animals.

Deloshekowa Ayyu'ya:nadinak'ya
REMEMBERING FAMINE

Years back, because of drought, some planted in hopes that the plants would grow for the people's survival. Some plants did grow a little with irrigation. People were worried why this was happening. In family homes people did wonder why this was happening.

Our main rich resource is corn. At the stores we can buy all kinds of produce and people think that there isn't famine, but there is. We can see it (hunger), but can't really admit it. Famine is within some homes where there are large families because our main food, corn, is not grown in abundance as it used to grow. We also don't store food for winter use. So people shouldn't waste food, they should eat well and be able to share.

Ko'lehoł Chummali Upchoyna'kya
HOW THEY GOT LOCUSTS

My mother would take a hoe and a bucket and go and dig out locusts. In the evening my mother would put the locusts in a bucket of water and soak them overnight. In the morning the locusts would be drained and washed. Locusts could be roasted in the black cooking pot and put in a bowl to eat. It had a great taste. My children used to fight over the meatier parts. My mother and Patricia's mother used to go out and dig out the locusts. This is what we ate as children.

— Margaret Edaakie

Chummali

LOCUSTS WITH CORNMEAL MUSH

3–4 SERVINGS
A bucket of locusts, about 4 cups
1 tablespoon cooking oil
1 cup white cornmeal
2 cups water
Salt, if desired

COLLECTING LOCUSTS:

Before the locusts spring out from the ground, take out a hoe and a bucket. Dig the locusts out, put them in the bucket, and cover the bucket with a cloth.

FIXING YOUR MEAL:

Wash the locusts. Heat oil in frying pan and toast the locusts until brown. It's ready when you smell a delightful taste. It's just like cooking pork chops. Set the locusts aside. Cook cornmeal in boiling water for 5–10 minutes. Place the locusts on a plate, the mush in a bowl, and there's your meal. You might serve some chiles on the side.

A young Zuni girl named Nita once said, "When I was done I asked what kind of meat they used for my sandwich and my family answered me, 'Well, what did you see being cooked in the frying pan?' To my surprise it was good. Remember this, ask about whatever you're being fed after you're full."

An elderly man and baby. Courtesy of the Smithsonian Institution.

SNACKS AND DESSERTS

NA'LE SHIK'USNA:WE
Deer Jerky

ALEKWI:WE DAP HE'SHO K'UWE I:YA'SENA
Parched Corn

K'OLA K'YAⱢK'OSENNE
Salsa

HE'BALOKYA
Whole Wheat Flour Pudding

Na'le Shik'usna:we
DEER JERKY

1 PIECE PER PERSON
Deer meat, leg and back are especially good for jerky.

DEER JERKY IS MADE only when a deer enters the home. Some body parts are given to family members. You would need to save a piece with a lot of meat on it in order to make jerky.

To make jerky, cut out a big chunk of meat and cut it in half, but not all the way through. Start to layer the meat that you cut in half by making thin slices of the meat. After you have sliced all the meat, hang it out on a line to dry. When dried it can be pounded into small pieces, fried, or made into soup with potatoes if desired.

Deer jerky is good, nutritious, and delicious.

K'ola Ma'chabi
USING CHILE PATTIES

Chile patties can be used at home, as well as by hunters. They can be taken along with non-perishable foods like parched corn, dried jerky, and dried peaches. Piki is also taken along with peanuts. Pieces of the chile patty are broken off to be eaten with the other foods to give them a delicious flavor.

Those that make the annual pilgrimage to Koluwala:w'a would take these kinds of food items. (See p. 82.)

Alekwi:wc dap He'sho K'uwe I:ya'sena
PARCHED CORN

25–30 SERVINGS (1 CUP PER SERVING)
2 cups of sand. Use clean, big grain sand. If you don't have a source for
    sand, it can usually be purchased at a lumberyard.
4 pounds mixed dried corn (white, blue and yellow) or one-color corn
2 pounds pinyon nuts, in the shell
(1½ pounds shelled pinyons can be used with the slight change in
    preparation noted below)
1 corn cob
½ cup salted water

MAKING OUTDOORS:

Build a fire. Place a cast-iron or other thick-clad pot about 6 inches above the ground and put in two or three cups of sand. When the sand gets hot put in your corn and pinyons. Stir the sand, corn, and pinyons* with a bundle of ¼″ dowel sticks until you hear the corn pop and the corn smells toasted, approximately 10–15 minutes depending on how hot your fire is.

Use a slotted dipper to sift out the sand. You have to be quick so that the corn won't burn. Put the roasted corn in a basket. Get a corn cob or a brush and dip it in the salted water to sprinkle the corn, and it's ready to eat.

*If you use shelled pinyons, add them to the sand and corn for the last five minutes of cooking time.

MAKING INDOORS:

Place your corn in a heavy pot and cook over a low heat on the stove. Stir with a wooden spoon until your corn pops. Add your pinyons as directed above.

DIPPERS

Zunis call anything they use as a ladle a dipper. This might be a traditional ladle or a small saucepan. In this case, you want an aluminum ladle or saucepan that is either slotted or that you have punched holes into to make it a sieve.

Do'y' An Doye:nak'ya
FARMING AT NUTRIA

WHEN YOU USED TO LIVE IN NUTRIA WHAT DID YOU PLANT?

We planted everything, mostly the shiny kind of corn. The corn we planted were the white corn, blue corn, mixed corn, red corn, and black. We also grew wheat and beans. We traded these mostly for other foods. It was the same way with the shiny corn too. Most of the food we planted was our daily food.

When my father was planting, he'd use a horse-driven plow and then wild potatoes would show up. We couldn't afford to buy potatoes so we just ate the wild ones that grew by our fields. The only time that they grew was when the ground was wet. In the spring-time when my father would be plowing, some potatoes would show up and I would go around and pick them up and put them in my bucket. I usually got around three buckets full. I would take them home and wash them. We'd boil them and then we would peel off the skin and eat them or sometimes we make stew with the potatoes.

— Lolita Edaakie

View of Upper Nutria, a Zuni farming village still occupied today.
Courtesy of the Smithsonian Institution. Photo by F. Krause.

K'ola K'ya l k'osenne

SALSA

8–10 servings
5 whole tomatoes
4 jalapenos or 4 yellow chiles
¼ of a bundle of fresh cilantro
3–5 cloves of garlic, depending on your preference
1½ cups water

WASH YOUR VEGETABLES. Break off the cilantro leaves from the stems and chop the vegetables so that it will be easier to put them in the blender. Blend to a chunky consistency. If you need a more spicy taste, add more chile. Same way with water. If needed, you can add more water too.

RAELYNN CACHINI '98 © ZUNI

He'balokya
WHOLE WHEAT FLOUR PUDDING

25–30 CUPS
12–13 pounds of whole kernel wheat or 5 pounds whole wheat flour
2 quarts water
2 cups sugar
1 cup panocha flour (germinated wheat flour, available in the
    specialty spice section of your grocery store)
cornhusks—2 bags or more

CLEAN AND WASH THE WHEAT and let it dry. Grind it into real fine flour. Or use your already ground flour.

Setting aside at least 2 cups of whole wheat flour, put the flour into a large dish pan. Boil the water. Pour the boiling water into the pan of flour and stir.

Now brown the sugar in the frying pan. Pour the sugar in the flour mix. While stirring, test to taste if it is sweet. Also at this time add the panocha flour. Keep adding hot water until it gets to be a thin batter. Stir in the last 2 cups of whole wheat flour to act as a binder. Now you can either put this batter in a casserole dish and bake in the oven or you can spread the batter on cornhusks and bake the filled husks in the oven. Bake at 350 degrees F for about 30 minutes until top is browned.

He'sho
WHOLE WHEAT CHEWING GUM

Wheat harvesting time is a time we looked forward to because our grandparents told us that chewing down on the wheat would turn into gum. We'd gather around where they would be threshing wheat. Cup in one hand, we would be gathering wheat until our cups were full. We would sit around munching on wheat and we actually would come up with chewing gum. It has a natural taste.

How would you feel about chewing wheat? It was hard to keep it together and at times you would end up swallowing the whole thing.

Two men, a woman, and some donkeys carrying goods on a street in the pueblo. Courtesy of the Smithsonian Institution.

THIS AND THAT

K'OLA MA'CHABI
Chile Patties

K'OLHEYA:WE
Chile Paste

K'E:TS'IDO'KYA K'YAⱢK'OSENNE
Tomatillo Paste

HA:K'YAWE
Native Tea

MOTS OBINNE
Sourdough Starter

ME:MOTS OBINNE
Yeast Starter

Ma'k'yayanne

SALT LAKE

I heard this story of the Salt Woman from my grandfather and other elderlies who used to tell it to each other.

What I know of how the Salt Lake got situated is that Salt Lake Mother was born to Mother Earth. Zuni Salt Lake was located east of the village where Blackrock Lake is now. Village people didn't respect the Salt Lake. Salt Woman decided to change her location because of immoral acts committed by the village people.

When Salt Mother left Blackrock things happened because of her supernatural powers. She penetrated through the rock cliff creating a large hole, called the Pierce Rock. She wore large fluffy eagle feathers as she was leaving for her new destination and one of her feathers fell off where it became a huge white rock that stands beneath Pierce Rock. Heading southward, she scattered cedar seeds where there is now a row of cedar trees.

There are a number of specific beliefs and rituals connected with Zuni salt. Zuni men and young boys that have been initiated into kivas are taken by their godfather's to get salt. Once there the young men are taught again of their religion. They plant prayer sticks and then they need to fast for four days. Coming home the godfather's family will do the purification rites and also the dividing of the salt among the families. Then the paternal aunts will do the same.

Salt that is being introduced into a home will be placed with an ear of corn. Prayers will be said for a long life. The Zunis believe that a chunk of salt placed near the newborn baby will protect the baby when it is by itself. Another belief is that if a chunk of salt is placed where food is kept, food will be plentiful as salt will never stop producing.

Salt can be used as a medicine because it contains the mineral sodium chloride. It can be used for washing out wounds and as a sore-throat gargle. Domesticated animals depend on salt. Salt is used in traditional cooking, preparing jerky, and general seasoning. Salt can also be used for tanning deer hides. Women are prohibited to go to the Salt Lake; it could cause leg cramps. Plant twigs dropped in the Salt Lake become crystals.

Salt is very sacred in our culture and one time we didn't have respect for the woman who shared her salt with our people, and for that she left us. Then she gave us another chance and we must not mistreat our chance at collecting salt from her. We must protect her and she will always be there. If we don't, she will leave us once again and this time won't come back.

K'ola Ma'chabi
CHILE PATTIES

6—8 PATTIES, 4 INCHES IN DIAMETER
12 red or green chile pods
½ cup of salt
1½ cups water (add more, if necessary)

PLACE RED OR GREEN CHILE, salt, and water in a blender and make a paste. Pour out about ½ cup for each patty on the hot griddle and brown on both sides. Place them on waxed paper, about an inch apart, on boards or a table to dry. Cover with waxed paper. Let dry thoroughly. Can be eaten with parched corn.

These store well in a sealed container for quite a long time.

K'olheya:we
CHILE PASTE

MAKES 2 CUPS
12 large chile pods; experiment with different varieties. Or use 2 cups
  of diced red chiles.
2 tablespoons dried cilantro seeds or ½ cup chopped cilantro leaves
1 or 2 cloves of garlic
1 cup water

TAKE THE STEMS OFF and roast the chile. Place chile, cilantro, garlic, and water in blender and whip to desired consistency. Add more water if paste is too thick.

K'eːts'ido'kya K'yaɫk'osenne
TOMATILLO PASTE
(WOLFBERRY)

MAKES 4–5 CUPS
6 to 10 tomatillos
4 or 5 pieces of roasted green chile for HOT paste, or reduce number
    of pieces to taste. (For a really HOT paste, add some diced
    jalapenos.)
fresh green onions for dipping

TOMATILLO PASTE IS MADE from green tomatillos that you gather or purchase. Boil the green tomatillos until the skins are loose. Peel the skins off and put the tomatoes and green chile together in a blender. Blend to a thick consistency. This is like a relish for steaks and also can be eaten as a dip with onions.

Some people like to eat tomatillos just plain.

Ko'hoʏ Leyadidun'ona A:ʏashshi A:wan A:ʏashshina:we A:beyekkowa Bena:we

PREDICTIONS THE ELDERS HEARD FROM THEIR PARENTS

The first prediction is that when your children watch television, they will see people doing bad things like killing, doing drugs, child abuse, abusing women, etc., that they will try to copy.

In the future dark fluids—meaning beer, wine or any kind of alcoholic beverages—will muddle your thinking and cause you to do bad things. People using these things will not treat other people right. Families will have problems.

When you are making rolling motions with your arms, hands, or fingers you would be told to stop because they say that you are softening mother earth.

When you are crying on the floor, you are told that you are crying for the Under Creature Uhe:bololo, because down in the Fourth World they would hear you.

During Deshkwi (a fasting period) you are not supposed to be hitting the ground because they say that you are are telling the creatures from the underworld to come up.

A ZUNI WOMAN AND CHILD. COURTESY OF THE SMITHSONIAN INSTITUTION.

Ha:k'yawe

NATIVE TEA

(THELESPERMA FILIFOLIUM AND MEGAPOTAMICUM)

1 BUNDLE MAKES 10 CUPS OF TEA
There are approximately 12 stalks in a bundle.

THERE ARE TWO DIFFERENT TYPES OF TEA. Both can be found growing around the Zuni fields. One of the two teas represents a boy, the Mołana and another to represents a girl, the Kya:naydu. Tradition says that if you are pregnant and you want a baby boy, start drinking the tea that represents the boy, the Mołana—and vice versa for a girl.

These wild teas are collected and bundled to dry, so when you ever want tea you can just boil the tea in water, add sugar, and enjoy.

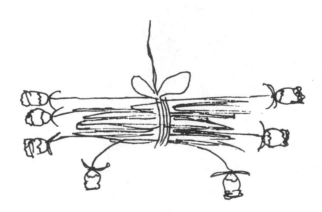

—ZUNI— 98 CLAYTON EDAAKIE ©

Mots Obinne
SOURDOUGH STARTER

MAKES ENOUGH STARTER FOR ABOUT 22 LOAVES OF BREAD.
4 cups water
1 scoop of starter, about golf ball size, saved from your last baking.
1 cup sugar
1 egg

MIX ALL INGREDIENTS TOGETHER. Add flour as needed to achieve the consistency of pancake batter. Let sit overnight.

Zuni bakers always save a quantity of starter from each baking session to have ready for the next time. If you do not have starter in your kitchen, commercial varieties can be purchased.

Me:mots Obinne
YEAST STARTER

MAKES ABOUT 3 CUPS OF STARTER, USE ABOUT 1 CUP OF STARTER PER LOAF.
2 cups warm water
1 package dry yeast
2 tablespoons honey
2 cups regular flour
(Some people also add 1 cup of shredded potatoes.)

Mix all ingredients together. Place in a warm spot and let sit overnight.

Kechiba
GYPSUM ROCKS-WHITE WASH

Gypsum comes in handy when cleaning walls. The rocks have to be soaked overnight. Before using it as paste, it will have to be checked for tiny pebbles by straining it through wire mesh. Also, the paste has to be drained before using. It is also used by a medicine society for body paint.

Ko'leho⎰ K'ola A:wakk'yana'dun'ona
HOW TO ROAST GREEN CHILES

Use care when roasting chiles. DO NOT put your fingers in or around your eyes as the chile will make them sting. Be sure and wash your hands thoroughly when done.

Chile can be roasted in the conventional oven or it can be roasted on hot charcoals.

Cover your oven rack with aluminum foil. Wash fresh green chiles. Prick chile with a fork on both sides. Place the chiles on the oven rack and put the rack in the lower broiler position. Broil until chile is blistered on one side. Turn the chiles over and broil until blisters form on other side and remove from oven.

Place cool, roasted chiles in plastic bags, getting as much air out as possible. Tie the bags well and put in freezer. Roasted chiles freeze well and can be stored in freezer for one year without losing their freshness. When needing to use chiles from freezer, defrost in bags or under lukewarm water. Then peel and remove the stems and seeds and use.

A MAN SITTING BY INDOOR FIREPLACE. COURTESY OF THE SMITHSONIAN INSTITUTION.

Dietary analysis

As Jim Enote states in the Foreword, the traditional Zuni diet has been radically altered by the introduction of non-traditional ingredients. The result has been a deterioration of the general health and well-being of the Zuni, especially evident in the widespread incidence of Type II diabetes.

In an effort to make Idonapshe an aid to the Zuni community in the preparation of healthy meals, the Zuni Diabetes Prevention Program conducted a dietary analysis of many of the recipes contained in this book. Cooks can use the analyses to monitor calories, fat grams, carbohydrates, and other nutritional contents in the foods that they prepare.

The Zuni Diabetes Prevention Program used "The Food Processor® Nutrition Analysis Software from ESHA Research, Salem, Oregon" to calculate the analyses.

SOURDOUGH BREAD (p. 6)

| Serving Size: | 67.51 g (2.38 oz-wt.) |
| Serves: | 220.00 |

Amount	Food Item	Weight (g)	Cals	Prot (g)	Carb (g)	Fiber (g)	Sugar (g)
0.11364 lb	All Purpose White Flour-Enriched-Bleached	51.55	187.63	5.33	39.33	1.39	0.88
0.00227 cup	Table Salt	0.65	0	0	0	0	0
0.00455 each	Dry Active Baker's Yeast-Package	0.03	0.09	0.01	0.01	0.01	0
0.01364 lb	Lard (Pork Fat)	6.19	55.79	0	0	0	0
0.03636 cup	Sourdough Starter	9.09	12.71	0.54	2.51	0.19	0.21
	Totals	67.51	256.22	5.88	41.85	1.59	1.08

Amount	Food Item	Fat-T (g)	Chol (mg)	Sodium (mg)
0.11364 lb	All Purpose White Flour-Enriched-Bleached	0.51	0	1.03
0.00227 cup	Table Salt	0	0	253.69
0.00455 each	Dry Active Baker's Yeast-Package	0	0	0.02
0.01364 lb	Lard (Pork Fat)	6.18	5.88	0
0.03636 cup	Sourdough Starter	0.05	0.05	2.03
	Totals	6.73	5.93	256.77

MILK BREAD (p. 7)

Serving Size:	61.41 g (2.17 oz-wt.)
Serves:	150.00

Amount	Food Item	Weight (g)	Cals	Prot (g)	Carb (g)	Fiber (g)	Sugar (g)
0.08333 lb	All Purpose White Flour Enrich-Bleached	37.80	137.59	3.91	28.8	1.02	0.64
0.06667 tbs	Baking Powder-Double Acting (Calumet)	0.92	0.49	0	0.2	0.00	0.00
0.02667 cup	Evaporated Whole Milk-Vit A Added-Cnd	6.72	9.00	0.46	0.6	0	0.67
0.01333 tsp	Table Salt	0.08	0	0	0	0	0
0.00667 tbs	Lard (Pork Fat)	0.09	0.77	0	0	0	0
0.06667 cup	Water	15.80	0	0	0	0	0
	Totals	61.41	147.85	4.37	29.7	1.02	1.32

Amount	Food Item	Fat-T (g)	Chol (mg)	Sodium (mg)
0.08333 lb	All Purpose White Flour Enrich-Bleached	0.37	0	0.76
0.06667 tbs	Baking Powder-Double Acting (Calumet)	0	0	97.52
0.02667 cup	Evaporated Whole Milk-Vit A Added-Cnd	0.51	1.98	7.12
0.01333 tsp	Table Salt	0	0	31.01
0.00667 tbs	Lard (Pork Fat)	0.09	0.08	0.00
0.06667 cup	Water	0	0	0.47
	Totals	0.96	2.06	136.88

Note

This recipe is divided into 15 loaves, NOT 15 servings!

Yellow Corn Meal Sweet Bread (p. 10)

Serving Size: 70.48 g (2.49 oz-wt.)
Serves: 10.00

Amount	Food Item	Weight (g)	Cals	Prot (g)	Carb (g)	Fiber (g)	Sugar (g)
0.2 cup	Yellow Cornmeal-Whole Grain	24.40	88.33	1.98	18.76	1.78	0.02
0.05 cup	All Purpose White Flour Enriched-Bleached	6.25	22.75	0.65	4.77	0.17	0.11
0.05 cup	White Granulated Sugar-Cup	10.00	38.70	0	9.99	0	9.99
0.3 tsp	Baking Powder-Double Acting (Calumet)	1.38	0.73	0	0.38	0	0.01
0.05 cup	Whole Milk-3.3% Fat	12.20	7.49	0.40	0.57	0	0.57
0.1 each	Raw Whole Fresh Egg-Medium-Each	4.40	6.56	0.55	0.05	0	0.05
0.05 cup	Water	11.85	0	0	0	0	0
	Totals	70.48	164.56	3.58	34.53	1.95	10.75

Amount	Food Item	Fat-T (g)	Chol (mg)	Sodium (mg)
0.2 cup	Yellow Cornmeal-Whole Grain	0.88	0	8.54
0.05 cup	All Purpose White Flour Enriched-Bleached	0.06	0	0.13
0.05 cup	White Granulated Sugar-Cup	0	0	0.10
0.3 tsp	Baking Powder-Double Acting (Calumet)	0	0	146.28
0.05 cup	Whole Milk-3.3% Fat	0.41	1.66	5.98
0.1 each	Raw Whole Fresh Egg-Medium-Each	0.44	18.70	5.54
0.05 cup	Water	0	0	0.36
	Totals	1.78	20.36	166.92

TORTILLAS (p. 12)

Serving Size:	104.20 g (3.68 oz-wt.)
Serves:	12.00

Amount	Food Item	Weight (g)	Cals	Prot (g)	Carb (g)	Fiber (g)	Sugar (g)
0.5 cup	All Purpose White Flour-Enriched-Bleached	62.50	227.50	6.46	47.69	1.69	1.06
0.33333 tsp	Baking Powder-Double Acting (Calumet)	1.53	0.81	0	0.42	0	0.01
0.08333 tsp	Table Salt	0.50	0	0	0	0	0
0.04167 cup	Instant Skim Dry Powdered Milk w/VitA	2.83	10.14	0.99	1.48	0	1.48
0.08333 cup	Water	19.75	0	0	0	0	0
0.08333 cup	Lard (Pork Fat)	17.08	154.09	0	0	0	0
	Totals	104.20	392.55	7.46	49.59	1.69	2.55

Amount	Food Item	Fat-T (g)	Chol (mg)	Sodium (mg)
0.5 cup	All Purpose White Flour-Enriched-Bleached	0.61	0	1.25
0.33333 tsp	Baking Powder-Double Acting (Calumet)	0	0	162.53
0.08333 tsp	Table Salt	0	0	193.79
0.04167 cup	Instant Skim Dry Powdered Milk w/VitaA	0.02	0.52	15.56
0.08333 cup	Water	0	0	0.59
0.08333 cup	Lard (Pork Fat)	17.07	16.23	0
	Totals	17.70	16.75	373.72

BLUE CORN PANCAKES (p. 13)

Serving Size: 67.94 g (2.40 oz-wt.)
Serves: 10.00

Amount	Food Item	Weight (g)	Cals	Prot (g)	Carb (g)	Fiber (g)	Sugar (g)
0.2 cup	Blue Cornmeal/AMI	24.40	89.30	2.37	17.47	2.39	—
0.05 cup	All Purpose White Flour Enrich-Bleached	6.25	22.75	0.65	4.77	0.17	0.11
0.05 tsp	Table Salt	0.30	0	0	0	0	0
0.15 tsp	Baking Powder-Double Acting (Calumet)	0.69	0.37	0	0.19	0.00	0.00
0.05 cup	Evaporated Whole Milk-VitA Added-Cnd	12.60	16.88	0.86	1.26	0	1.26
0.1 cup	Water	23.70	0	0	0	0	0
	Totals	67.94	129.30	3.87	23.69	2.56	1.37

Amount	Food Item	Fat-T (g)	Chol (mg)	Sodium (mg)
0.2 cup	Blue Cornmeal/AMI	1.10	0	0.98
0.05 cup	All Purpose White Flour Enrich-Bleached	0.06	0	0.13
0.05 tsp	Table Salt	0	0	116.27
0.15 tsp	Baking Powder-Double Acting (Calumet)	0	0	73.14
0.05 cup	Evaporated Whole Milk-VitA Added-Cnd	0.95	3.70	13.36
0.1 cup	Water	0	0	0.71
	Totals	2.11	3.70	204.58

BLUE CORN MEAL PATTIES (p. 16)

Serving Size:	84.35 g (2.98 oz-wt.)
Serves:	10.00

Amount	Food Item	Weight (g)	Cals	Prot (g)	Carb (g)	Fiber (g)	Sugar (g)
0.4 cup	Blue Cornmeal/AMI	48.80	178.61	4.73	34.94	4.78	—
0.15 cup	Water	35.55	0	0	0	0	0
	Totals	84.35	178.61	4.73	34.94	4.78	0

Amount	Food Item	Fat-T (g)	Chol (g)	Sodium (mg)	(IU)	(mg)	(mg)
0.4 cup	Blue Cornmeal/AMI	2.20	0	1.95			
0.15 cup	Water	0	0	1.07			
	Totals	2.20	0	3.02			

FRY BREAD (p. 17)

Serving Size:	130.32 g (4.60 oz-wt.)
Serves:	12.00

Amount	Food Item	Weight (g)	Cals	Prot (g)	Carb (g)	Fiber (g)	Sugar (g)
0.33333 cup	All Purpose White Flour-Enriched-Bleached	41.67	151.67	4.31	31.79	1.13	0.71
0.33333 tsp	Baking Powder-Double Acting (Calumet)	1.53	0.81	0	0.42	0	0.01
0.08333 tsp	Table Salt	0.50	0	0	0	0	0
0.04167 cup	Whole Milk-3.3% Fat	10.17	6.24	0.33	0.47	0	0.47
0.08333 cup	Water	19.75	0	0	0	0	0
0.125 lb	Lard (Pork Fat)	56.70	511.43	0	0	0	0
	Totals	130.32	670.16	4.64	32.69	1.13	1.19

Amount	Food Item	Fat-T (g)	Chol (mg)	Sodium (mg)
0.33333 cup	All Purpose White Flour-Enriched-Bleached	0.41	0	0.83
0.33333 tsp	Baking Powder-Double Acting (Calumet)	0	0	162.53
0.08333 tsp	Table Salt	0	0	193.79
0.04167 cup	Whole Milk-3.3% Fat	0.34	1.38	4.98
0.08333 cup	Water	0	0	0.59
0.125 lb	Lard (Pork Fat)	56.66	53.87	0.01
	Totals	57.41	55.25	362.74

MIDALIK'O (p. 27)

Serving Size:	300.88 g (10.61 oz-wt.)
Serves:	8.00

Amount	Food Item	Weight (g)	Cals	Prot (g)	Carb (g)	Fiber (g)	Sugar (g)
0.5 cup Raw-Cup	Purslane (Khursa)-	21.50	3.44	0.28	0.74	0.17	–
0.1875 cup	Whole Grain White Cornmeal	22.87	82.81	1.86	17.59	1.67	0.02
1.0625 cup	Water	251.81	0	0	0	0	0
0.03125 cup	Hot Green Chili Peppers-Raw Chopped-Cup	4.69	1.88	0.09	0.44	0.07	0.23
	Totals	300.88	88.12	2.23	18.77	1.91	0.26

Amount	Food Item	Fat-T (g)	Chol (mg)	Sodium (mg)
0.5 cup	Purslane (Khursa)- Raw-Cup	0.02	0	9.68
0.1875 cup	Whole Grain White Cornmeal	0.82	0	8.01
1.0625 cup	Water	0	0	7.55
0.03125 cup	Hot Green Chili Peppers-Raw Chopped-Cup	0.01	0	0.33
	Totals	0.85	0	25.56

FRIED SUMMER SQUASH (p. 30)

Serving Size: 112.11 g (3.95 oz-wt.)
Serves: 8.00

Amount	Food Item	Weight (g)	Cals	Prot (g)	Carb (g)	Fiber (g)	Sugar (g)
1 cup	Meas Raw-Trimmed: Summer Squash (All Varieties) Slices-Bld	105.30	21.06	0.96	4.5	1.4	
0.03125 cup	Soybean Oil (Crisco/Wesson)	6.81	60.22	0	0		
	Totals	112.11	81.28	0.96	4.5	1.4	

Amount	Food Item	Fat-T (g)	Chol (mg)	Sodium (mg)
1 cup	Meas Raw-Trimmed: Summer Squash (All Varieties) Slices-Bld	0.33	0	1.05
0.03125 cup	Soybean Oil (Crisco/Wesson)	6.81	0	0
	Totals	7.14	0	1.05

BEEF STOMACH - TRIPE (p. 34)

Serving Size:	434.35 g (15.32 oz-wt.)
Serves:	12.00

Amount	Food Item	Weight (g)	Cals	Prot (g)	Carb (g)	Fiber (g)	Sugar (g)
0.08333 kg	Beef Tripe-Raw	83.33	81.67	12.17	0	0	0
0.08333 cup	White Hominy-Canned	13.75	9.90	0.21	1.97	0.34	0.08
0.08333 gal	Water	316.00	0	0	0	0	0
0.75 oz-wt	Chile Paste	21.26	9.55	0.49	2.22	0.34	1.15
	Totals	434.35	101.11	12.87	4.18	0.69	1.23

Amount	Food Item	Fat-T (g)	Chol (mg)	Sodium (mg)
0.08333 kg	Beef Tripe-Raw	3.29	79.17	38.33
0.08333 cup	White Hominy-Canned	0.12	0	28.88
0.08333 gal	Water	0	0	9.48
0.75 oz-wt	Chile Paste	0.06	0	2.03
	Totals	3.47	79.17	78.72

MUTTON POSOLE STEW (p. 36)

Serving Size:	361.46 g (12.75 oz-wt.)
Serves:	15.00

Amount	Food Item	Weight (g)	Cals	Prot (g)	Carb (g)	Fiber (g)	Sugar (g)
0.13333 lb	Meas Raw Boneless: Lamb Chop-Arm Choice-1/4"Trim Braised	47.78	165.32	14.52	0	0	0
0.13333 lb	Hominy-Cooked	60.48	53.22	1.27	12.34	3.45	—
0.06667 tsp	Table Salt	0.40	0	0	0	0	0
0.06667 gal	Water	252.80	0	0	0	0	0
	Totals	361.46	218.54	15.79	12.34	3.45	0

Amount	Food Item	Fat-T (g)	Chol (mg)	Sodium (mg)
0.13333 lb	Meas Raw Boneless: Lamb Chop-Arm Choice-1/4"Trim Braised	11.47	57.34	34.40
0.13333 lb	Hominy-Cooked	0.73	0	107.05
0.06667 tsp	Table Salt	0	0	155.03
0.06667 gal	Water	0	0	7.58
	Totals	12.19	57.34	304.07

Note

This recipe also calls for 1 lb. soup bones.

CHILE STEW WITH POTATOES (p. 40)

Serving Size:	552.54 g (19.49 oz-wt.)
Serves:	7.00

Amount	Food Item	Weight (g)	Cals	Prot (g)	Carb (g)	Fiber (g)	Sugar (g)
0.28571 lb	Meas Raw: Beef Stew Meat-Cooked-Lean & Fat	79.06	240.73	21.95	0	0	—
0.28571 tbs	Soybean Oil (Crisco/Wesson)	3.89	34.41	0	0	0	—
1.14286 cup	Water	270.86	0	0	0	0	—
1.14286 each	Meas Raw: Peeled Potato-Boiled w/o Skin-Each	154.50	132.87	2.66	30.90	2.78	1.5
1.56 oz-wt	Chile Paste	44.23	19.85	1.03	4.61	0.71	2.4
	Totals	552.54	427.87	25.64	35.51	3.50	3.9

Amount	Food Item	Fat-T (g)	Chol (mg)	Sodium (mg)
0.28571 lb	Meas Raw: Beef Stew Meat-Cooked-Lean & Fat	16.30	78.94	231.95
0.28571 tbs	Soybean Oil (Crisco/Wesson)	3.89	0	0
1.14286 cup	Water	0	0	8.13
1.14286 each	Meas Raw: Peeled Potato-Boiled w/o Skin-Each	0.15	0	7.73
1.56 oz-wt	Chile Paste	0.11	0	4.23
	Totals	20.46	78.94	252.03

DEER JERKY SOUP (p. 42)

Serving Size:	231.17 g (8.15 oz-wt.)
Serves:	12.00

Amount	Food Item	Weight (g)	Cals	Prot (g)	Carb (g)	Fiber (g)	Sugar (g)
0.04167 lb	Venison Jerky-4 inch strip	18.90	64.51	6.41	2.79	0	—
0.16667 tbs	Soybean (Hydrogenated) & Cottonseed Oil	2.27	20.07	0	0	0	0
0.33333 cup	Peeled Potato-Diced-Boiled w/o Skin-Cup	52.00	44.72	0.89	10.40	0.94	0.52
0.66667 cup	Water	158.00	0	0	0	0	0
	Totals	231.17	129.30	7.31	13.19	0.94	0.52

Amount	Food Item	Fat-T (g)	Chol (mg)	Sodium (mg)
0.04167 lb	Venison Jerky-4 inch strip	2.91	25.87	553.39
0.16667 tbs	Soybean (Hydrogenated) & Cottonseed Oil	2.27	0	0
0.33333 cup	Peeled Potato-Diced-Boiled w/o Skin-Cup	0.05	0	2.60
0.66667 cup	Water	0	0	4.74
	Totals	5.23	25.87	560.73

PINTO BEAN SOUP (p. 45)

Serving Size:	430.40 g (15.18 oz-wt.)
Serves:	6.00

Amount	Food Item	Weight (g)	Cals	Prot (g)	Carb (g)	Fiber (g)	Sugar (g)
0.16667 lb	Pinto Beans-Raw	75.60	257.04	15.80	47.93	18.45	3.78
0.16667 tsp	Table Salt	1.00	0	0	0	0	0
0.08333 lb	Cured Pork Bacon-	37.80	217.73	11.53	0.22	0	0.22
1.33333 cup	Water	316.00	0	0	0	0	0
	Totals	430.40	474.77	27.33	48.15	18.45	4.00

Amount	Food Item	Fat-T (g)	Chol (mg)	Sodium (mg)
0.16667 lb	Pinto Beans-Raw	0.85	0	7.56
0.16667 tsp	Table Salt	0	0	387.58
0.08333 lb	Cured Pork Bacon-Cooked	18.60	32.13	603.29
1.33333 cup	Water	0	0	9.48
	Totals	19.45	32.13	1007.91

BLUE CORN SOUP (ATOLE) (p. 51)

| Serving Size: | 333.72 g (11.77 oz-wt.) |
| Serves: | 8.00 |

Amount	Food Item	Weight (g)	Cals	Prot (g)	Carb (g)	Fiber (g)	Sugar (g)
1.34375 cup	Water	318.47	0	0	0	0	0
0.125 cup	Blue Cornmeal/AMI	15.25	55.81	1.48	10.92	1.49	—
	Totals	333.72	55.81	1.48	10.92	1.49	0

Amount	Food Item	Fat-T (g)	Chol (mg)	Sodium (mg)
1.34375 cup	Water	0	0	9.55
0.125 cup	Blue Cornmeal/AMI	0.69	0	0.61
	Totals	0.69	0	10.16

BLUE CORN TAMALES (p. 54)

Serving Size:	137.50 g (4.85 oz-wt.)
Serves:	12.00

Amount	Food Item	Weight (g)	Cals	Prot (g)	Carb (g)	Fiber (g)	Sugar (g)
0.83333 cup	Hominy-Cooked	137.50	121.00	2.89	28.05	7.84	–
	Totals	137.50	121.00	2.89	28.05	7.84	–

Amount	Food Item	Fat-T (g)	Chol (g)	Sodium (mg)
0.83333 cup	Hominy-Cooked	1.65	0	243.48
	Totals	1.65	0	243.48

FRESH SWEET CORN TAMALES (p. 56)

Serving Size:	122.00 g (4.30 oz-wt.)
Serves:	6.00

Amount	Food Item	Weight (g)	Cals	Prot (g)	Carb (g)	Fiber (g)	Sugar (g)
2 each	Gr. Giant Corn on the Cob Nibblers PLB	122.00	13.42	3.66	27.69	2.44	4.88
	Totals	122.00	13.42	3.66	27.69	2.44	4.88

Amount	Food Item	Fat-T (g)	Chol (mg)	Sodium (mg)
2 each	Gr. Giant Corn on the Cob Nibblers PLB	1.10	0	10.98
	Totals	1.10	0	10.98

DEER JERKY (p. 72)

| Serving Size: | 14.00 g (0.49 oz-wt.) |
| Serves: | 1.00 |

Amount	Food Item	Weight (g)	Cals	Prot (g)	Carb (g)	Fiber (g)	Sugar (g)
1 piece	Venison Jerky- 4 inch strip	14.00	47.78	4.75	2.07	0	—
	Totals	14.00	47.78	4.75	2.07	0	—

Amount	Food Item	Fat-T (g)	Chol (mg)	Sodium (mg)
1 piece	Venison Jerky- 4 inch strip	2.16	19.17	409.92
	Totals	2.16	19.17	409.92

WHOLE WHEAT FLOUR PUDDING (p. 77)

| Serving Size: | 136.53 g (4.82 oz-wt.) |
| Serves: | 30.00 |

Amount	Food Item	Weight (g)	Cals	Prot (g)	Carb (g)	Fiber (g)	Sugar (g)
0.16667 cup	Whole Wheat Flour-Baked Value	20.00	67.80	2.74	14.52	2.44	0.40
0.06667 quart	Water	63.20	0	0	0	0	0
0.06667 cup	White Granulated Sugar-Cup	13.33	51.60	0	13.32	0	13.32
40 g	Wheat Sprouts	40.00	79.20	3.00	17.00	0.44	–
	Totals	136.53	198.60	5.74	44.84	2.88	13.72

Amount	Food Item	Fat-T (g)	Chol (mg)	Sodium (mg)
0.16667 cup	Whole Wheat	0.38	0	1.00
0.06667 quart	Water	0	0	1.90
0.06667 cup	White Granulated Sugar-Cup	0	0	0.13
40 g	Wheat Sprouts	0.51	0	6.40
	Totals	0.88	0	9.43

CHILE PASTE (p. 82)

Serving Size:	309.60 g (10.92 oz-wt.)

Serves:	1.00

Amount	Food Item	Weight (g)	Cals	Prot (g)	Carb (g)	Fiber (g)	Sugar (g)
2 cup	Hot Red Chile Peppers-Raw-Chopped-Cup	300.00	120.00	6.03	28.41	4.50	15.93
2 each	Fresh Garlic Cloves-Each Measure	6.00	8.94	0.38	1.99	0.13	0.10
2 tbs	Dried Coriander/ Cilantro Leaf	3.60	10.04	0.79	1.88	0.37	0.75
	Totals	309.60	138.98	7.20	32.27	5.00	16.77

Amount	Food Item	Fat-T (g)	Fat-S (g)	Chol (mg)	A-IU (IU)	Vit C (mg)	Sodium (mg)
2 cup	Hot Red Chile Peppers-Raw-Chopped-Cup	0.60	0.06	0	32250.00	729.00	21.00
2 each	Fresh Garlic Cloves-Each Measure	0.03	0.01	0	0	1.87	1.02
2 tbs	Dried Coriander/ Cilantro Leaf	0.17	0.00	0	210.60	20.41	7.60
	Totals	0.80	0.07	0	32460.60	751.28	29.62

CHILE PATTIES (p. 82)

Serving Size:	129.94 g (4.58 oz-wt.)
Serves:	8.00

Amount	Food Item	Weight (g)	Cals	Prot (g)	Carb (g)	Fiber (g)	Sugar (g)
1.5 each	Chile Pepper-Raw	67.50	29.87	—	—	—	—
0.0625 cup	Table Salt	18.00	0	0	0	0	0
0.1875 cup	Water	44.44	0	0	0	0	0
	Totals	129.94	29.87	0	0	0	0

Amount	Food Item	Fat-T (g)	Chol (mg)	Sodium (mg)
1.5 each	Chile Pepper-Raw	—	—	3.17
0.0625 cup	Table Salt	0	0	6976.44
0.1875 cup	Water	0	0	1.33
	Totals	0	0	6980.94

SUGGESTED READINGS ABOUT ZUNI

CUSHING, Frank Hamilton
Zuni Breadstuff, Museum of the American Indian, Heye Foundation: New York, 1920

DUNMIRE, William W. and Gail D. Tierney
Wild Plants of the Pueblo Province, Museum of New Mexico Press: Santa Fe, 1995

FERGUSON, T. J. and E. Richard Hart
A Zuni Atlas, University of Oklahoma Press: Norman, 1985

HUGHTE, Phil
A Zuni Artist Looks At Frank Hamilton Cushing, Pueblo of Zuni Arts and Crafts and the A:shiwi A:wan Museum and Heritage Center: Zuni, 1994.

NAHOHAI, Milford and Elisa Phelps
Dialogues With Zuni Potters, Zuni A:shiwi Publishing: Zuni, 1995

OSTLER, Jim, Marian Rodee, and Milford Nahohai
Zuni: A Village of Silversmiths, Zuni A:shiwi Publishing: Zuni, 1996

STEVENSON, Mathilde Coxe
"The Zuni Indians: Their Mythology, Esoteric Fraternities, and Ceremonies." *23rd Annual Report of the Bureau of American Ethnology for the Years 1901–1902.* Washington, D.C., 1904.

WYACO, Virgil
A Zuni Life, The University of New Mexico Press: Albuquerque, 1998

INDEX